T0208665

In a Million Years

rse books may be ordered through booksellers or by contacting:

rse
iberty Drive
ington, IN 47403
universe.com
Authors (1-800-288-4677)

978-1-4502-7350-3 (sc)
978-1-4502-7351-0 (ebk)

l in the United States of America

rse rev. date: 03/30/2011

NEVER IN A MILLION

SYLVAN MARLI

iUniverse, Inc.
Bloomington

NEVER IN A MILLION YEARS

THE COVER AND CONTENTS OF

THIS BOOK

IS THE EXCLUSIVE PROPERTY OF

SYLVAN MARLER

For more copies of:

NEVER IN A MILLION YEARS

WRITE OR CALL YOUR REQUEST TO:

SYLVAN MARLER

37 TEMPLE AVE.

FORT WALTON BEACH FL 32548

HOME PHONE: 850-243-2465

IN MEMORY OF:

My Father, William L. "Bill", "Papa Bill" "Pop" Marler

My Mother, Sibyl S. "Mama Sibyl" Marler

And my wife Shirley's father and mother

Joe and Florence Baker

DEDICATED TO:

Shirley B. Marler, My Sweet Wife of over 56 Years

For her support and Inspiration

And our two Daughters and Families:

Jo Elaine Bilby, Husband Ken and their 3 Sons

Jonathan and Wife Elisabeth

David and Wife Tara

Michael and Kristina

Mary Mills and her Husband Anthony

APPRECIATION TO:

To the Lord God above for choosing my wife, Shirley and
Myself, before the foundation of the World, to be Man and Wife
for almost 57 years. And a wonderful life it was!

NEVER IN A MILLION YEARS

TABLE OF CONTENTS

THE W. L. MARLER FRONT OVERLOOKING EAST PASS & GULF

NEVER IN A MILLION YEARS

ABOUT THE AUTHOR

SYLVAN MARLER spent 8 months and 28 days in Destin, Florida, before birth! On October 14th, 1923, Sibyl Marler, his Mother, with birth pains growing closer and closer, was placed in a motorized net boat by his father, William L. "Bill" Marler and RUSHED to the nearest Hospital, 7 hours away, to Pensacola, Florida, 49 miles to the west (a 7 hour boat ride)!. It wasn't an easy trip 7 miles over Choctawhatchee Bay, 35 miles up Santa Rosa Sound and 7 miles over Pensacola Bay! But 3 days later, on October 17, 1923, in the Pensacola Hospital, little baby Sylvan decided to make his debut into this world of woe! Five days later he moved back to Destin, with his Mother and Dad, to begin his journey through life! Except for his absence from 1942 to 1947, he spent his entire life in the Destin-Fort Walton Beach Area!

Sylvan Marler has written 4 books besides "NEVER IN A MILLION YEARS",

They are:

"WHO IS THIS MAN CALLED JESUS CHRIST"

"PRECIOUS DISCOVERIES" 1971 being revised

"SELLING SIGNS SUCCESSFULLY" not marketed

"GATEWAY TO DESTINY" 2001 in print

"GATEWAY TO DESTINY II" 2004 in print

4

NEVER IN A MILLION YEARS

INTRODUCTION

"NEVER IN A MILLION YEARS" is a true and delightful story of a young lady and a young man whose love stemmed out of two small villages over 1450 miles apart.

The young lady, Shirley Baker was born in Elgin, Nebraska on January 1, 1935. She and her parents Joe and Florence Baker moved to Neligh, Nebraska, along with the rest of her family, when she was a very young child to the home shown below, where her parents lived the rest of their lives.

The young man, Sylvan Marler, was bornin Pensacola, Florida on October 17, 1923. Shortly after he was born, he and his parents went back to their home in Destin, Florida, a small fishing village in the Florida Panhandle, on the Gulf of Mexico where they lived for many years in the home shown in the picture below.

NEVER IN A MILLION YEARS

FOREWARD

NEVER IN A MILLION YEARS is a true and wonderful love story about a young couple that lived over 1400 miles apart and that were destined to meet each other in Destin, Florida one day.

The circumstances of how they met is so unusual that it boggles the mind. It is as though, that, it happened by divine providence, a greater power than human nature could plan it. It was phenomenal, extraordinary and highly remarkable!

A true love story that is so wonderful and amazing that it seems too good to be true! BUT, IT IS!!

THIS WONDERFUL AND AMAZING LOVE STORY BEGINS NEXT........READ ON..........

NEVER IN A MILLION YEARS

Destin, Florida—June 1951

June of 1951, Mr. Mark A. Hienselsman, and his wife Margie were on vacation in Destin, Florida from Webster Groves a Suburb of St. Louis, Mo. He planned his vacation so that it would coincide with the Destin Gulf Coast Fishing Rodeo which ran the entire month of June. The Rodeo was in its third year of existence, having begun in June of 1949. Each year, the Hienselman's stayed at the Marlborough Motel and Cottages, owned and operated by W. L. "Bill" and Sibyl Marler the father of Sylvan Marler. Sylvan owned and operated his own business of sign making, known as Sylvan Signs in Ft. Walton until 2007. Ft. Walton and Destin are about 7 miles apart. Many afternoons, after work,

Sylvan would drive over of Destin to visit his parents and meet and talk to some to the Motel and Cottages Guests.

The Marler property was on the water facing the Destin Harbor & Gulf of Mexico. See drawing below.

The guest and visitors would sit under the beautiful, swept back oak trees in the cool evening gulf breeze, chat and look at the beautiful gulf and watch the many boats coming and going.

While Sylvan was visiting with the guests, He and Mr. Hienselmans got pretty well acquainted over the several evenings.

A Lonely Life

On the last evening of Mr. Hienselsman's vacation, Mr. Hienselman said to Sylvan. "Sylvan, my wife and I have grown fond of you. You seem to be a nice young man. Next year, when we come to Florida we're going to bring our 17 year old Daughter, Marcia, with us, so that she can meet you!" Sylvan was excited about that. Sylvan, by this day in time was in his mid twenties and had lived a fairly lonely life, trying to find the right girl of his dreams, so far, without success. Sylvan said to Mr. Hienselman, "That would be nice, I would like to meet her!"

Like most young men, Sylvan had dated many young ladies over the past few years, but they never turned out exactly right for him. You see, Sylvan had made up his mind a long time ago that, marriage was forever, and you had to have the right one in order for that to work out.

You readers might ask, in your mind, "What does Mr. Hienselman have to do with a young lady in Nebraska and a young man in Florida and a young lady in St. Louis, Mo.?" And the answer is "very special!"...Just read on...and you will see!

Let's take a trip up to Neligh, Nebraska and look in on Shirley Baker and family. The Bakers were Farmers and Cattle Ranchers. They raised cattle, planted and grew corn, wheat and Alfalfa.

When Shirley was a young girl she had inherited an allegoric skin disease, from her father, known as Eczema. If not medically controlled it causes the skin to itch all over and sometimes becomes red and scaled. (The disease turned out to be a life long affliction). Her Mother, Florence, took her to several local Doctors over several years, without much help. It was recommended by one of the Doctors that she be taken to Mayo Bros. Clinic in Rochester, Minn., for testing. In the early spring of 1951 Mrs. Baker called Mayo Bros. Clinic and set up an appointment. Meanwhile, over in Webster Groves, a suburb of St. Louis, Missouri, Marcia Hienselman, as a young girl, was, also, plagued with a disorder similar to that of Shirley Baker. Her mother, also, set up an appointment with the Mayo Bros. Clinic at the same time, (Now bear in mind, that, these two families had never met before and, consequentially, did not know each other before this event).

A Visit to Mayo Bros. Clinic

Shirley and Florence, her mother, arrived at Mayo Clinic around mid-April of 1951. After registering Shirley at the Clinic, Shirley was assigned to a room with two beds. Florence checked in to a Boarding House near the Clinic.

Meanwhile, Margie and Marcia arrived at Mayo Bros. Clinic on the same day. When Marcia was registered in at the Clinic, she too, was assigned a room. In the other bed in the same room that Shirley was in! This is not too unusual, normally. However, in this case it is amazing and unusual. Margie, Marcia's mother, checked in to the same Boarding House as Margie. Shirley was 16 years old at that time and Marcia was around 17. It would be a very important to note here, that, Sylvan would never have met Shirley if she, and Marcia had not had similar diseases!

During their stay at the Clinic, Shirley and Marcia became very close friends as did Florence and Margie. Shirley invited Marcia to come out to their farm in Nebraska and visit that summer, in 1951. During their correspondence that year, Marcia invited Shirley to come over to visit her, in St. Louis, the following summer in 1952. In one of her letters, during the spring of 1952, Marcia told Shirley, "Mom

9

and Dad want to take me to Destin, Florida for a couple of weeks in June. Check with your folks and see if it is alright for you to go with us to Florida." Shirley wrote Marcia a few days later, "Mom and Dad said it would be O. K. and I am so excited, I can hardly wait!"

Vacation in Destin

Late Thursday afternoon, June 5, 1952, The Hienselmans and Shirley Baker checked in to one of the cabins at The Marlborough Motel & Cottages in Destin, Fl. where the Hienselmans always stayed.

A Cordial Meeting

On Friday afternoon, June 6, the day after the Hienselmans and Shirley arrived in Destin, Sylvan went over to visit, late in the afternoon, as usual, and to meet Marcia Hienselman. Charles Davidson, A close friend and X-Brother in law of Sylvan's and X Son-in-law of Bill and Sibyl Marler, was, already, visiting the Marlers and the guests, that evening, on the hill overlooking the Destin Harbor and the beautiful Gulf of Mexico, when Sylvan arrived. Sylvan got out of his car and walked up to where the Hienselmans were sitting. Mr. Hienselman arose and introduced Sylvan to Marcia and Shirley Baker. Marcia and Shirley were as different as night and day. Marcia was a beautiful blonde, vivacious, outspoken Betty Hutton type (Betty Hutton was a beautiful Blonde, vivacious Comedian & Singer/Dancer in the late forties and through the fifties) and Shirley was a beautiful brunette, quiet spoken and a sweet looking, dignified type young lady. Just the type Sylvan had been looking for. As a matter of fact, about two years before this, Sylvan had had a dream of being married to a brunette young lady, by the name of Shirley, who would meet him at the door each evening after work. Sylvan attributes the name Shirley to the fact that he was so fond of Shirley Temple in the earlier days.

Well, let's get back to the meeting on the hill over

looking the beautiful Gulf of Mexico and the boats going to and fro such as this nice little schooner pictured at left. Also, pictured below, is the Marlborough Motel and Cottages on which the hill is located. The Cabin in the middle bottom of the picture is the one in which the Hienselmans were staying on their vacation.

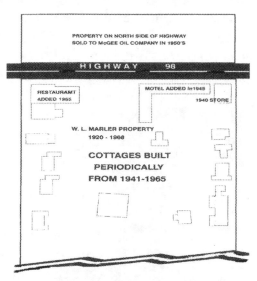

PROPERTY ON NORTH SIDE OF HIGHWAY
SOLD TO McGEE OIL COMPANY IN 1950'S

HIGHWAY 98

RESTAURANT
ADDED 1965

MOTEL ADDED In 1945

1940 STORE

W. L. MARLER PROPERTY
1920 - 1966

COTTAGES BUILT
PERIODICALLY
FROM 1941-1965

The pictures below at left, is Mama Sibyl Marler. The one at right is Capt. Papa "Bill" Marler, owners of the Marlborough. Also the Mother and Father of Sylvan Marler. (Taken around 1947).

After Sylvan, Charles, Marcia, Shirley and the Hienselmans chatted for a while. Sylvan spoke up and asked, "Would you girls like to take a ride down by the gulf and walk on the beach for a little while?" Marcia ask, "Mom and Dad, would it be O. K.?" excitedly. "Yes, but don't stay too long."

As the four of them got close to Sylvan's car, Shirley ran and jumped into the front seat beside Sylvan. Charles and Marcia sat in the back, of course!

As the two couples walked along the Gulf shore a few feet apart, Sylvan Asked Shirley, "Shirley, are you from St. Louis too?" Oh, no!" replied Shirley, I am just visiting Marcia there, I'm from Neligh, Nebraska", continued Shirley. Neligh? Where is that?" asked Sylvan. "It's a small farming town

about 150 miles Northwest of Omaha on Highway 275." Shirley Replied.

The two couples spent about half hour to forty-five minutes walking on the beach, then returned to the Marlborough and chatted a while longer. During that time, plans were made to go out, Saturday night, to a drive-in restaurant, in Fort Walton, for a sandwich and a "Coke".

They spent Sunday evening sitting in front of the cottages, talking and enjoying the balmy breeze blowing in off the Gulf of Mexico.

How about a fresh Seafood Dinner

The following Monday night the two couples drove all the way to Pensacola, fifty miles west, to have a seafood dinner at the famous Firehouse Seafood Restaurant on East Gregory St.

The seafood served at the Firehouse Restaurant was the freshest seafood served anywhere. "The seafood that they served, today, slept in the Gulf last night!" Sylvan doesn't know what Charles and Marcia had that night, but, Shirley and Sylvan ordered fresh Gulf Red Snapper. It was hot, fresh, and delicious!

Shirley said, "I have never liked the fish that I have had back home, but that was superb." She was hooked on fresh Florida Gulf seafood. Since that first Seafood Dinner, Shirley eats fresh Gulf seafood every chance she gets!

Sylvan and Shirley spent several evenings alone, just to talk and get to know each other better. A couple evenings they went to a movie at the Tringas Theatre in Fort Walton. One of those nights they saw "The Lady in Red" starring Jane Powell.

Every one of these evenings together seemed to bring their lives closer knit to each other.

Some of those evenings alone, Sylvan would sing some love songs to Shirley, Such as:

"NEVER IN A MILLION YEARS"

"Never in a million years could there be another you.

I would shed a million tears, if ever we were through.

There would be no world for me, if every should we should part.

Where I go your name will be, Right on the tip of my heart.

Only once in every lifetime, someone just like you appears.

There couldn't be another you, never in a million years."

And others, like....."Darling, you and I", "Beautiful Dreamer", "Yours", "Indian Love Call", "Ah, Sweet Mystery of Life", "It's a sin to tell a lie", Etc.

Some evenings Sylvan and Shirley talked about their future, together. They felt like their love was real, and was here to stay.

On Tuesday evening, June 17, was an emotional evening. Shirley was leaving the next morning. They would not see each other, again, for several months and, maybe, not forever! Only the future would tell! Sylvan said to Shirley, "Shirley, you are a wonderful, sweet young lady. I like you very much. As a matter of fact, I think I love you very much. I can see that, your parents have raised you up right. I'll bet they are very proud of you. You are going to make some man a wonderful wife, someday. I hope and pray that man will be me." I like you very much, too, Sylvan I, also, believe I love you." Shirley Replied. "Yes, my parents have been wonderful to me, and taught me to do right" added Shirley

Plans were made for Sylvan to travel to Nebraska, in September, to visit Shirley and meet her Parents and family. They promised to write each other as often as possible.

"Well it's time to say goodbye. Parting is such sweet sorrow and I'm going to miss you very much!" Sylvan said to Shirley. "I'm going to miss you, too, Sylvan!" replied Shirley, Sadly.

They embraced, kissed, and said goodbye. Shirley went into the cabin and Sylvan drove back to Fort Walton with heaviness of heart and Shirley on his mind.....to stay.

The next few months, Sylvan worked around his business with a very lonely heart.

COURTSHIP BY MAIL

The days, weeks and months ahead were going to be long and lonely ones. Sylvan was, already, planning ahead for September, putting a little money aside for that September trip to Nebraska.

Late Saturday afternoon, June 21, Sylvan was working in down town Fort Walton, across from the Post Office, and decided to pick up his mail before he went back to the shop. Among his bills and other mail was the beautiful, welcome, envelope below:

He got into his truck, opened and read the following letter, three times

June 18, 1952

My Dearest Sylvan,

Now that I have a chance to write, the words just won't come. All day long I've been thinking of you and different things to tell you, but now, nothing sounds right.

We left about six o'clock this morning, and arrived here just before dark. It was a very trying trip and I am, truly, as tired as I have been in a long time. The bed looks mighty good, but I had to, at least, say hello to you.

It certainly will seem like years before I hear from you. I know, though, that you will be thinking of me as often as I think of you. Oh, September, hurry and come! Isn't that right? Will close now and hope to hear from you soon.

Yours Truly,

Shirley

P. S. I'm crazy about you!

As soon as Sylvan read the letter, several times, he was so excited he could hardly wait until he got home to answer Shirley's letter.

Sylvan lived in a small one bedroom, concrete block house that he had built for himself on a 100' x 200' lot that he had purchased in 1950 at 330 Elliott Road on Elliotts Point in East Fort Walton.   That evening, Sylvan answered Shirley's letter.

Fort Walton, Fla.

June 21, 1952

My Dearest Shirley,

This afternoon about dusk, I was working across the street from the Post Office. Some thing kept telling me to go over to the Post Office and get the mail. I had been wanting to go all day, but I knew I couldn't possibly have a letter from you, yet. But I went, anyway.   Boy! I sure was happy when I saw the letter from you.   You can't imagine how I have missed you...   Right away I sat right down in the truck and read it 3 times. I could hardly wait until I got home to answer it. Well here I am.

The past four days have seemed like an eternity. If four days seem so long, what will 21/2 months seem like before I see you again 10 long weeks. I will be counting the days until Sept. 10th.

Sweetheart, if your folks like me like my folks like you, I will be very happy. They think you are sweet. All of them like you very much, but not as much as I do, Nobody could, Shirley, please don't change, because....

Never in a million years could there be another you. I would shed a million tears, if ever we were through. There would be no world for me if ever we should part. Where I go your name will be, right on the tip of my heart. Only once in every lifetime, someone just like you appears. There couldn't be another you, never in a million years.

It's only a song, but, a beautiful one, and it comes from deep inside, believe me. I think of you every minute of the day. I don't guess I'll ever feel the same about anyone else, I know I won't. Darling, like you, there are lots of things I want to say, but, I just can't seem to think of them now.

Boy! Will I be working a lot harder for the next year. Working harder to get farther ahead to make things happier for the future. A future, I hope will include you. A year from now will tell the answer. A long drawn out year of eternity!

Shirley, I'm a little undecided whether to send it to your home or to you in care of Marcia. Tell the Hienselmans hello for me, will you? I will send it to you there and you will get it quicker. If you have already gone home, they will send it to you.

Again, Shirley, I say I miss you very much and can hardly wait to hear from you. Thanks for writing so soon. I am happy and unhappy. Happy because I *heard from you and unhappy because you are not here in person,*

Yours very truly,

Sylvan

P. S. I'm crazy about you, too!

Shirley went over to Lebanon, Ill. To spend a couple days with her older Brother, Roger, and his new bride, Joan, right after she and the Hienselmans arrived back in Webster Groves. (Her brother was in the military service and was stationed at Scott Air Force Base. Roger and Joan were Married just before Shirley left on her vacation in 1952).

That day, after arriving at her brothers, Shirley wrote her second letter to Sylvan.

June 23, 1952

My Dearest Sylvan,

I imagine you have received that terrible letter by now. I was so tired that night, but, I had to, at least, say hello. Sylvan, I thought of you, that day, all day long and I haven't stopped yet. I have a feeling that you are doing the same, but would give anything to hear from you.

I'm spending a couple of days at my Brother and Sister-in-law's home. They were married just before I left on my vacation. Roger is stationed at Scott Air Force Base and they have a lovely apartment here in Lebanon.

We arrived in St. Louis about midnight Thursday. We rode through the Ozarks Thursday and it was really beautiful. I wouldn't advise you to take that route unless you aren't in a hurry. I rather have the idea you will be in a hurry, am I right?

As I mentioned, back a ways, I'm dying to hear from you, but I don't know when, for I'm not, at all, sure when I will be home. I thought I might be home Thursday or Friday, but now, my brother thinks he is going home the 4th, so, I might wait. I plan on calling the folks tonight, so will spend most of my time here because the Hienseleman's will tire of me, if they aren't already. What do you think? How are you and all of the other folks back in Florida? I wish I were there. Tell everyone hello, but especially Little Mother.

I don't believe I told you, Chuckie finally kissed me good

bye, four times! (Chuckie was Charles Davidsons six year old son). He's learning young, don't you think? Sylvan, please excuse the stationary for beggars can't be choosers. (I mean I am the beggar, for I got it from Jo, my sister-in-Law). Sylvan, I must close now for my Mother will feel bad if I don't write a few lines. Bye now Sylvan

Yours

Shirley,

Dearest ---I phoned home just a while ago and couldn't get anybody. I'm going to try again tomorrow. I'm not at all sure, but, I think I will stay, so write me here. If I'm not here when your letter gets here, Joan will send it on. The address is:

Box 112

Lebanon, Illinois

Hope you can half way read my writing. I'm not going to make any excuses for I can't help it one bit.

Now that I have started writing again, I can't stop, so, you will just have to put up with me. Think you can stand it? I hope so. It has really been hot today, but I've been enjoying myself, thoroughly. Roger and Jo's apartment is very nice, but, the thing I enjoy is doing something besides loafing. It was fun, but I really enjoy doing a little cooking and cleaning once again.

Sylvan, how is the sign painting business coming along? I hope you aren't working too hard. I wouldn't want you to kill yourself. That last sentence doesn't sound like it should. I take it, that, you know what I mean. Would it be better if I addressed your letters Box 638 instead of % Sylvan Signs? I better close again for Jo has some visitors.

Always yours

Shirley

P. S. Crazy about you!

A couple of Sylvan and Shirley's letters crossed in the mail before Shirley returned back home to Neligh, because they were so anxious to talk to one another, they couldn't wait to get the next letter from each other. Sylvan's next letter to Shirley was written on June 25, before he received an answer to his first letter. Here it is:

Box 638
Ft. Walton, Fla.

June, 25 1952

My Dearest Shirley,

I find it just a little difficult to wait a week to write you again, therefore, I'm going to say hello sooner than you expected. I sent my first letter to St. Louis, or rather to you in care of the Hienselman's in Webster Groves-- - But, will send this one to your home. Hope you received the other letter O. K. How was the trip? Did everything go all right? (Please excuse the writing. I have a pen here that scratches). I left my own pen at the shop. I am home for lunch, I fixed my own. Little Mother is still in Pensacola. I will, probably, go and get her one night this week. (Little Mother is Sylvan's Grandmother.) Would you like to go with me? I'll sing you a few songs, like "Never in a million years", "Beautiful Dreamer", "Memories", "Indian Love Call", "Ah, sweet mystery of life" and many others. Aw, c'mon, go with me, we'll have fun.

I went to the wrestling matches, last night, with Dad. I didn't care about going, because, wrestling is usually fixed, but, it was a benefit bout, so, Dad twisted my arm. Tonight, I will go to the stock car races. They changed them from Sunday afternoons to Wednesday nights.

Shirley, when does school start in Neligh?

I heard that Charlie is coming back to Florida, <u>to stay</u>, in a couple weeks. Won't that be nice? The only thing bad about it is you and Marcia won't be here.

Sweetheart, the past week and one day have seemed like forever and a day, time is passing so slow.

I was hoping you would write me, again from Webster Groves, but, I guess you were too busy and too tired, from your, trip, to write. I sure hope to hear from you real soon. Have you told your folks about me yet? Don't forget the date I ask you about, I want to send it off as soon as I can.

I have already started to save for my vacation in Sept. I can hardly wait until then. I sure hope you still want me to come by that time. Will you? I wonder!

Well, my sweet, I guess this brings me to the end of another boring letter from that fellow in Florida. Please keep your letters coming. I will answer every one that you write.

Yours very truly,

P. S. I'm, still crazy about you!

Shirley received the letter that Sylvan wrote her on June 21 five days later in the late afternoon of June

26, while she was back in Webster Groves with Marcia. The following is her answer:

June 27, 1952

My Dearest Sylvan,

I received your letter, yesterday, and nothing could have made me happier than that, but seeing you. I would have gotten it Wednesday, but as you know, by now, I was visiting my brother. If you were to send it to their address, my Sis will send it along. Sylvan, when I speak of a sister, you will know I'm talking about a sister-in-law, for I have no sisters. I have four brothers, three older and one younger. I'm slipping in a few details about my family so you will not have such a hard time keeping them straight this September. I guess your lesson is complete for today, but, believe me, there shall be more.

Dearest forgive this pencil, Marcia can't seem to find a pen. I sort of have the idea that you wouldn't mind if it were written in crayon. I know, that is the way I feel.

Darling, I thank you for writing me that beautiful song. I could practically hear you singing it. It made me feel so good and so very close to you. Darling, I'm positive that there never will be another you.

Dearest I'm very happy that your family likes me, for they are wonderful people. Please don't worry about my family, for I can't see how they could help liking you. I couldn't help it even if I was foolish enough to want to.

Today we went on an excursion boat, the S. S, Admiral, and I had quite a nice time. I would have had a super time if only you had been with me. I didn't stop thinking that very thing for one minute. I think of you all the time, but something like that really makes you think it isn't fair.

Darling, it's getting late and I had better close. Once again, though, I miss you terribly. I'm waiting for September to come around with you.

I realize I said I must close, but that is as hard as saying goodbye. I haven't much more to say, but it seems we aren't so many miles apart when I'm writing to you or reading a letter from you. Believe me, I shall be reading that precious letter every day until I get your next one!

Is September 10th a definite date? We start school the first week in September, but never worry, that shall not get in the way. Dearest, after using all this paper, I remember, I forgot to tell you, I'll be home by, at least, Wed. You said you had to, (I should say, are going to) work harder for a better future. I, too, hope it contains me. If not, I am afraid I shall be very unhappy.

Now, Sylvan, I must, certainly, close.

Yours very truly

Shirley

P. S. I hate to waste so much paper, so will tell you one more time that I miss you very much, in fact, I'm crazy about you!

June 29, 1952

My Dearest Sylvan,

Did you enjoy the stock car races today? Or didn't you go for some reason? If it was as hot there as it was here in St. Louis you were better off at home.

I have a letter, here, for you that I wrote Friday night. I believe I will send it along with this, even if it is a mess. Marcia couldn't, for the life of her, find a fountain pen that night and tonight about a dozen of them turned up. I did, really, intend to mail it before now, but due to circumstances, was unable.

Darling, from now on, you can address all letters to dear ole' Neligh, for I am going home tomorrow. It will seem wonderful to be with my family and friends again. It could be perfect only if you were to be there too. Sylvan, how about another lesson on the Baker family? No, I guess I shall wait to see if you like the idea. Just now, I am listening to an advertisement (I guess I had start—egad! Let's just forget I ever started to say anything. I guess the T. V. is what distracted me.

These slanting lines look silly, don't they? I am writing on, just a book, so that accounts for some of it.

Sylvan, darling, remember what you promised to write me? Well, get busy, and tell me who said it, I'm

26

extremely curious. I must close for Marcia is through writing Lawrence and is ready to gab. Don't forget that I miss you very much and will be thinking of you every minute.

Yours truly,

Shirley

On June 26, Sylvan wrote his third letter to Shirley In answer to her second letter, that, had arrived after he had come home from work that day. He sent it to Shirley in care of her brother in Lebanon, Ill. It arrived there after Shirley had left for home and it was forwarded to her in Neligh.

Ft. Walton, Fla.

June 26, 1952

My Dearest Shirley,

I was working in Santa Rosa today and didn't get home until about eight o'clock tonight. Boy, was I pleasantly surprised with your second letter staring me in the face. This is my third letter to you.

I sure hope you have received my first one as I sent it to Webster Groves in care of the Hienselman's and Lebanon is only 25 miles from their home. I mailed it to you last Monday morning, before eight o'clock. You should have gotten it Tuesday or Wednesday, had you been at the Hienselman's as I mailed it air mail. The second letter, I sent to your home. I wrote it last night as I just couldn't wait until I heard from you again, to write as you will see in that letter. Boy! Do I miss you and, I, also, think of you every minute of the day, believe it or not. Of course, I know that you believe in me, or else you wouldn't care for me as you do, and I know you do, because I care for you. Isn't it funny, how we hit it off, right a way? I sure hope it was meant to be that way, and I hope it will, always be that way. I, also, hope there won't be any obstacles standing in the way. Of course, I know, that if, it is real love there can be no obstacles, right? The first letter you wrote me <u>was not terrible.</u>

It was wonderful! You couldn't ever know how happy I was just to get even the P. S. on that letter, believe me.

It makes me very happy to know that you are thinking of me almost as much as I think of you.

Boy! I can't keep up with you, sweetheart. First, I hear from you in Memphis, Then, I write you in St, Louis, then, I write to you in Neligh, Now, I'm writing you in Lebanon, Ill. Boy, you sure do get around, don't you? It sure is nice that you are spending a few days with your brother and sister-in-law. I hope you have a swell time, and don't you go home until you get this letter. But, then, you had better get home so I can keep up with you. (I'm kidding, of course). I kind of feel bad, with me getting all the letters and you not getting any. But, you will. They'll probably be piling up on you and you'll start getting bored from hearing from me.

How could anyone tire of you, anytime? I know I would never tire of you and I don't think the Hienselman,s would, either.

Listen, Pal, you can bet your last cent on me being in a hurry, when I come to Neligh in Sept. Yes, I will be, and I won't take that route, if it takes longer. As a matter of fact, a friend of mine in Santa Rosa, who spent most of his life in that section, said he would draw out the quickest route for me, when I told him I was going to Nebraska on vacation in Sept. And I told him I wished to get there as soon as I could. He'll fix me up as soon as I am ready to go.

All the folks here are getting along fine. I wish you were here, too! You'll be here someday, maybe to live...Eh???? As I told you, in my first letter, my folks, all like you very much. Dad thinks you are a very nice girl. Mother thinks you're really sweet and likes you lots. She said, "You seemed to like us very much!" Little Mother says, "She's an awfully sweet girl!" Rose, Carmen, & Sibyl says, "She's sweet, sensible and adorable!" and I think there aren't enough words in the dictionary to describe you! So there! (Rose and Carmen are Sylvan's sisters and Sibyl Rose is Sylvan's first cousin).

Yes, you told me, on the telephone, that day, that Chuckie kissed you goodbye. He told me, too. Dog-gone-it and you wouldn't even let me kiss you! Rose, went out the door a few minutes ago as I was starting this letter. She says to tell you hello. So, Hello Shirley! I told you in my letter before, that, Little Mother is still in Pensacola. Well, she isn't back yet. She, also, would say hello. Boy! When I get started writing, it is hard to stop me. Don't get bored! Listen, Darling, make no excuse about your writing or your stationery. Just keep the letters coming. If you write them on a throw-a-way match cover, I'll still be happy to hear from you. As far as your writing is concerned, I love it! As you said, you couldn't help it. You write the way you write, I write the way I write and hang what anyone else thinks about it. Just write! I would sit down and read your letter if you wrote a whole newspaper. I won't, ever, get bored believe me!

Shirley, the sign painting business is good. I keep busy, all day. I never seem to get caught up. I'm hoping it will start to slack up soon. It does get tiresome, and, that vacation won't be before I need it, believe me, as I haven't taken one day off at a time in over three years. I went to Birmingham in Sept. 1949 and stayed with some relatives for a week. I had a pretty good time, but, I know it will never compare with the vacation I'm going to have this Sept. I have already started saving for it, as I told you in my letter before.

My Darling, I can't let up on my work, too much, in the next year as I want to clear off some of my indebtedness before next _June_ Then, maybe life will begin without too much worry. This fall, I will start subdividing my large piece of property and start selling the lots to pay off some of my bills. It wouldn't take much though. But, I will try my best not to kill myself in my work. My vacation, this Sept. will add another few years to my life, believe me.

Shirley, dear, it wouldn't really matter how you addressed my letters, I will still get them, just the same. Box 638 or care of Sylvan Signs or both, or just Sylvan Marler, I'll get them. I sure did enjoy your letter. I have read it several times, you signed your letter "Always Yours", I hope you really mean that. Forever, I mean. I would like to have you always, Honest! Well, darling, It's closing time again and I'll say goodnight until I hear from you, again. There are many things I would say to you, if you were here.

Always Yours.

Sylvan

P. S. I'm still crazy about you, too.

P. P. S. Can you top this?

Sylvan hasn't received a letter in several days, so he decided not to wait to get Shirley's next letter before he wrote her and send it to her home in Neligh......

July 1, 1952

Ft. Walton, Fla.

My Dearest Shirley,

It has been almost a week since I heard from you last and I just couldn't wait until I hear from you again to write.

Darling, it was just 2 weeks ago, tonight, that I last saw you, but it seems like centuries. I'll probably go crazy before Sept. if it is like this all the way through the next 2 months. Yes, in 2 months I'll be packing my things and getting ready for the trip, that is, if you still want me to come by then?? Gee whiz, Shirley, I sure will be glad when you are home so that we can get on a regular schedule with our writing. I miss you so much and each one of your letters is just like a shot in the arm, they keep me going another day or so! I want to hear from you so often that if I heard from you every day,, I'd still want one twice a day, I know you are real busy, though, and I can't write too often. I am going to try and write one in the middle of the week and one on Sunday. That way you will get one on Saturday and one about Wednesday. Would that be all right? Well, I guess you will be home by the time this letter gets there. I hope so! Evidently, you haven't received my first letter yet, or hadn't received it last week. I sent it to Marcia's home. I sure hope you have gotten all of my letters by now. Because, if you feel the way I do, the waiting is unbearable. Isn't that right? Perhaps you don't feel the same!

I am hoping to hear from you tomorrow, Wednesday. I've got to.

I guess you are wondering why I am changing my page numbering, and going from one page to the next instead of the usual English way? Well, I figure, this way is more like a book and will be easier for you to read without shifting Back and forth, and when I get into some of my long letters, you won't have too much trouble holding on to the paper. It is possible they will prove boring, but, when I like someone, a lot, I can have lots of nothing to say. Maybe I'll say the same things over and over again. You can't ever tell about me. I'll think of something, if it takes all night. When I'm writing you I have all night and tomorrow too, if I wish to take it!

Shirley Dear, tell me something about your section of the country. Is it hilly and mountainous? Or, is it low and flat like a plain? I'll bet it is really beautiful there. It must be, because, cattle grazing country is usually beautiful. Does your Dad's farm border on the Elkhorn River? What about the Elkhorn River? Can you swim in it? Is there good fishing there, such as Brim and Rainbow Trout? Tell me something about the town of Neligh. I know it has 5,000 inhabitants. I suppose the chief industry, naturally, would be cattle. What kind of entertainment does it have, excluding Bars and Saloons, as you know, I don't care for them! What kind of nice hotels or rooming houses do you have? With reasonable rates, of course, as I can't afford too steep prices, because of the future plans that I have. I want to take you to a few places. Nothing but the best for you!

Little mother is back from Pensacola. I went in Saturday night. I thought of you being with me if only in spirit, and I did sing a few songs to you. Little Mother and I talked about you, nice things, of course. She said that she sure wishes she had gotten to know you better. She's in bed right now. Gee whiz, I sure wish you could have been with me. It was lonely without you.

I told you that Charlie was coming back to stay. He will live in Pensacola with my Uncle and manage one of his businesses for him. Then he can be near Chuckie, or, at least, he can see him more often. (Something is happening to my pen).

Chuckie and the other kids were over to my house Sunday. I told Chuckie that you told me he kissed you goodbye and he said "yes". I said, "She is really nice, isn't she?" He said, "Yes" He said "do you like her?" and I said "Yes, an awful lot". He said, "Do you love her?" I said, "I'm not sure, but I think so!" He said, "Are you going to marry her?" I said, I might, if she wants me next year, or the year after, You can't tell about those things!" That ended that conversation. He's really a smart boy. We are proud of my Nephew aren't we, Shirley, Dear?

Well, my sweet, the end of another journey through memory lane. Maybe, some day all these things will be true...and maybe not. Who knows what the future brings. It brings sadness and good cheer, May our happiness last through eternity. God will guide us.

"Good night, Sweetheart"

"Be my love..."

"Yours, forever"

Sylvan

P. S. I'm still crazy about you!!!

On Wednesday July 2 Sylvan received Shirley's third and fourth letters that she had written on June 27 and June 29, together. Here is his answer:

Box 638

Ft. Walton, Fla.

July 2, 1952

My Dearest Shirley,

I received your third letter today and your fourth one included from St. Louis. Boy, what a happy fellow after waiting almost a week. It seemed like years since the last one and now since you are home, we don't have to wait so long to get that well needed boost to the next one. Every sentence in your letters make me feel very happy and proud that I have a sweetheart as sweet, kind and

35

so wonderful as you are. Stay that way just for me, will you?

I am very happy that you finally got a letter from me. I knew you would get one sooner or later, but, it didn't seem like you would, the way you have been moving around and thank goodness you are getting them as I wrote them... I'll always be proud of you, my Dear, in every way. The one and only one who will ever keep me happy at all times.

I, too, could never be happier then when I receive your letters except to see you in person. Oh, happy Day, please hurry!

Yes, I did send a letter to your brothers, but you have gotten it by now and several more, besides. Isn't it wonderful? I mean to get letters from someone, whom you love, so very much, so dearly!

Yes, My Darling, I do want to know all about your family. You don't have to tell me they are wonderful, because, they would have to be to have a daughter and sister like you. I know they are. I do want to know them all, very much. Are all your brothers at home, except Roger?

You can give me a lesson in every letter, if you wish. I'll enjoy it immensely. Shirley, Dear, I really wouldn't mind what you wrote your letters with, as long as you write them. I care for you, just as you are!

"Never in a million years" will always be our theme song, through the years to come, right? I, also, am positive that there will never be another you, and there'll never be another for me, but you! I sure am happy that you can't help liking me, I hope you'll always feel that way, for 100 years or more. I know I'll always feel that way about you.

It would have been wonderful if I could have been with you on the excursion on the S. S. Admiral. We, both, would have had a super time.

I miss you, My Darling, almost more than I can bear. It is so hard waiting and waiting for so long a time to see you. It will be so very wonderful when we can be together again.

I'll be there with Sept. as it rolls around, believe me, if it is in my power.

Gee whiz, dear, you say you must close and I'm wishing you

wouldn't. I could sit and read your letters all night! If I got ten a day, I'd still read them all before I stopped, believe me.

It does seem as though we're not quite so far apart when I am writing you, or, reading one of your letters, but, oh, how I wish there weren't more than an inch between us. I would be the happiest man on earth today.

(This darn pen, I'm going to throw it away and get a new one).

No, Shirley, Sept. 10th is not, definitely, a set date. As a matter of fact, the set date is as follows: I'll leave Ft. Walton on the third, which is Wednesday. It is possible that I will arrive in Neligh on Friday if all goes well. That will give me Sat. and Sunday with you, If possible. Also, the whole next week, after school, and the following weekend. I will leave Sunday, Sept. 14, in the evening or early Monday, Most likely Monday morning. That will give me two weekends with you, if you can stand me that long. You'll probably get tired of me the first weekend. Yes? My future, from now on, will include you, My Darling. I know you'll be good for me. I know our future will be a very happy future. I'll do my best to keep you the happiest girl in the world. My love for you will grow through the years.

Well, Shirley, I have come to the end of an almost perfect day. It would have been perfect if you were with me. Your letter made it almost perfect.

I miss you every minute of the 24 hours each day and think of you just as much.

Forever yours

Sylvan

P. S. Still crazy about you!

July 2, 1952

My Dearest Shirley,

I received another letter from you a few minutes after I wrote the other Letter I just couldn't wait over another minute to answer your last letter of the 27th (Sunday). I didn't go to the stock car races last Sunday as they have been changed to Wednesday nights, instead. I went tonight, though. In fact I just got home at 10:45 p.m. It is exactly 12:00 midnight. I'm still going to answer this letter of yours. Your other letter was not a mess. It was beautiful. I mean it. Yes, isn't it wonderful that I can address all your future letters to good 'ole Neligh. I sure am happy that you are home. I'm with you at all times even if it is only in spirit. We will count the days until I will be there with you in flesh. Yes, Darling, I say bring on the lesson on the Baker family. I really want to know every one.

Yes Shirley, Darling, I do remember what I promised to write you. I was wondering when you were going to get around to asking me.

Well, Little Mother told me that Marcia had her eyes on Charlie. I think Mother must have told Little Mother and possibly, Carmen told Mother. Boy, Things like that sure do get around, don't they? That is the way it's got to me. Of course, Marcia was just having a good time. But, she did like Charlie quite a bit, but everyone does. Isn't that right? He's always jolly, kind and considerate.

I'm not forgetting, for a minute, that you miss me and are thinking of me every minute, as I am doing the same. It will be a glorious day when I can just reach out and touch you. Boy, what a day that will be! Sweetheart, you'll have to give me some instructions on what to do the first day I get to Neligh. I wish, very much, to see you, first, for a few minutes before I meet your family. If it is not at all advisable, then I'll be content just to see you with all the family at the same time. What ever is best, that's what I'll want.

It is exactly 63 days until I'll see you. Come on days, let's see you fly by.

Yours eternally,

Sylvan

P. S. I'm more crazy about you!

Sylvan didn't hear from Shirley for several days, after the last letter, so, on Sunday, July 6, he decided to sit down and write a short letter to say hello:

July 6, 1952

Ft. Walton, Fla.

My Dearest Shirley,

I know you didn't get home until sometimes Wed. so, You couldn't have had time to write in time for me to get a letter from you yesterday (Sat.) I sort of expected one, but it didn't come. I know I'll get one tomorrow, though. I thought I'd say hello, tonight. I worked on our house nearly all day today. I'm finishing up the little room on the back of my house.

I will sleep back there instead of in the living room, like I have for the past year. Then, the living room will be converted into a living room, like it should be. My Sister and Little Mother sleep in the bedroom, as you know. I will be doing a lot of work on the house before next year. You won't know it when you see it again.

Shirley,, my Darling, I am still counting the days until Sept. 6, when I will see you again. Oh happy day! Exactly, 2 months, or 61 days. They are dropping slowly, but surely. It isn't as bad as it was, is it?

I look forward to your letters as though it were you coming, and I feel like you are right beside me, when I am reading your letters. I wish you were! As far as I am concerned, I'll always feel the same as I do now, and, my future plans all contain you, the sweetest girl in the world. I really mean that. Thank your mother and father for me, will ya? for being such wonderful people. They must be for they have a wonderful Daughter. I know I said this before, but, I want you to know that it comes from the heart.

Shirley, Dear, send me a picture of you. Will you? I would like to have one of your, family, if it is possible, and it won't be too much trouble. If you don't already have one, I can wait until I meet them.

I am planning to have some pictures made and when I do, I'll send you the best one, although the best one might scare you!

Well, Sweetheart, I'll say Goodnight, for now, and try to answer your next letter as soon as I get it. I will go to the Quarterback club meeting tomorrow night.

Always yours

Sylvan

P. S. I'm still crazy about you!!!

Shirley arrived home about 1:30 on Monday June 30. The letter that Sylvan had sent to Lebanon, Ill. Had been forwarded on to Neligh and was waiting for her when she got home. Then, the next morning, July 1, Sylvan's last letter had arrived. Shortly after Shirley arrived home, she told her mother about Sylvan. I would like to explain something to you readers. Shirley was 17 years old and would be graduating from High School in May 1953. She was a very sensible and wise young lady, wise, far beyond her age. Sylvan was 28 years old and younger than his age. However, the age difference would cause problems with her parents as well as her young lady friends, until the initial shock wore off and they, all, found out more about Sylvan in the months to come, and that Shirley and Sylvan truly loved each other, and no one but the God above could change that, for it was his purpose and plan for them to meet. <u>It was, truly, a match made in Heaven!</u>

Shirley started her answer to Sylvan's last letters on July 1, 1952.

After the first two pages it was interrupted by some sad and, almost unbearable circumstances for Shirley. Here is her sad and heart breaking letter:

Neligh, Nebraska

July 1, 1952

My Dearest Sylvan,

I arrived home about 1:30 and found a letter from you just waiting for me and nothing could have pleased me more, believe me. Then, this morning, I received your 3rd letter, which my sister had sent on. so, you can't imagine how happy I've been!

Yes, Sylvan, I would love to go to Pensacola with you. I'm positive I would, I mean we would, have a grand time. I'm sure I would enjoy all those songs, but, especially, "Never in a million years." which we both love. It should be our song, don't you think?

You asked when school starts. I believe I told you all I know in letter no. 3. Usually, the first Monday in Sept. Don't worry about it, though, for we can arrange things somehow.

Darling, isn't it grand, June is finally passed? Let's hope July passes faster.

Won't that be wonderful if Charlie can live in Florida. It will be a very nice thing for Chuckie, everything straight in line. You know, truthful and sincere, especially.

Sylvan, don't even think, for one minute, that your letters could ever be boring.

Sylvan, I'm like you, I can't wait a week to write the next letter. It seems I just finish writing one and I could sit down and write another.

Darling, I'm glad you realize I believe in you, for I do and I also feel that you believe in me. Yes, it is funny how we hit it off, right away. Funny but nice! Like you, I hope it was meant to be that way, and that there won't be any obstacles standing in the way.

Shirley's letter was interrupted for several hours by a visit from her girl friends and a talk with her mother.

My sweet darling, about 5 hours ago my girl friends came out to see me and so your letter was interrupted. Just those 5 short hours ago I was very happy because I had your letters and I was writing to you. Now I am so very sad and it is hard to bear. Much worse, you will have to suffer, also.

Another lapse of time.

I've seen broken hearts over children who forget their Mothers and Fathers love them dearly and Sylvan, now there has been another lapse of time and things are looking brighter. Mother wanted me to go up to the other farm, with her, to get Dad and we had another talk, which makes things better. They, still aren't as good as they might be, but, not as bad either. I realize you would

44

like to know what happened, and I will try to get it across to you. When I talked to Mother this morning, I tried to give her the truth, then, I told my girl friends about you and the age made them exclaim loudly and laugh. They're very young, yet, if you understand what I mean.. After they left, Mother had me sit down and have a talk. She had been worrying because, if you can understand, I'm her only girl and she has things planned out for me. Better things than she had a chance for, and I'm still too young, in her eyes. Things got down to where we shouldn't even write anymore. I guess I was able to get through to her, that I did have some sense, and I most certainly didn't have any idea about not finishing school, and a few other things.

Sylvan, Darling, imagine what torture I've been going through. I <u>couldn't</u> give you up completely and I could hardly be terrible to my parents. I took it quite hard and knew it would be terrible trying to tell you. Now that I have talked to Mother again, I find it to be, that, she has her trust back in me, again. It boils down to the fact that, it would be better if you waited until next year, about this time, to come see me. I know this all sounds like everything is impossible, for I have been feeling the same way, too. But, after thinking, I know, if we both care, that in the end, it will work out. We can still write one another.

Believe me, my Darling, this is hurting down deep and if you can understand, things may, I mean, can work

45

out. I feel you will understand, for you are the kind, sweet person who would.

I fear that I must go through nurses training for reasons I will try to make you understand another time. I believe you can feel the way I'm feeling now, so, I won't try to explain all.

So, my Sweet Darling, if you can see waiting until graduation, which is next May, to see me and try to work things out, it will make things a little better. Sylvan, please try to stop and think things over and don't get completely depressed as I did at first. Please try not to think, bad, of my parents for they have made me what I am. And (I could hardly just) omit. A person can't just kick parents in the rear and tell them to go to----when they find a new life. Do you see what I am trying to say? My folks are grand people and you will love them, too. I have to do things the way they think best for their certain child. My darling, I feel I should close for things are getting harder and harder to explain. I just want to say that the very last thing I would want to do on this earth is to hurt you. For what hurts you, hurts me even more.

Always yours
Shirley

P. S. I sincerely believe that both of us should speak to our Dear Lord quite often about these things.

P. P. S. Write me as soon as you can see things clear.

Sylvan received Shirley's sad letter on July 7th about 2 hours after he had mailed his last letter to her. He went home at lunch time and answered it and had it in the mail by 4 p. m. that same day, HERE IT IS:

July 7, 1952

Ft. Walton, Fla.

My Dearest Shirley,

I received your 4th letter today, which contains both, happiness and sadness. It hurts me deeply because you are sad, even for a minute. I don't want you to feel sad or downhearted, even for that one minute.

I really don't have to think it over before I write. You see, My Darling, I am not, completely, surprised by your Mothers re-actions, for I had anticipated as much. I understand, thoroughly, how they feel. It is a natural reaction, and you must try to believe, that, what your parents say or do, for you, is for the best and, that, they really don't want to hurt you! It's just like you said, things are not as bright as they could be, but it's always darker before the dawn. The way your parents feel about the situation could not make me like them any less, as your parents have been here a lot longer than either of us, and 90% of the time, parents are usually right. Their advice to us is not to hurt us, but, to make us see the light in every way, the good in something, as well as the bad! They have been through these things, before, and know, almost, what the outcome will be. Believe in your Mother, my Dear, and she will try to guide you through the bitter and sweet.

I know it looks very dark now, but there is an old saying,

"In to every life some rain must fall." Interpreted, "In to every life some tears must fall." The sun shines brighter after each rain. Remember that. Also, remember that after a years time, if we both feel the same, and, it is Gods will that we be life companions, it will be so! What is to be, shall be! I'm sure, if your parents see that you still feel the same in a year or so, They, too, will be just as happy as you want them to be!. So, My Shirley, please cheer up, and, believe me, everything will turn out for the best. Remember, I believe in you and you believe in me. And that is the biggest thing of all. We must be content and as happy as can be until we see each other.

Maybe my standards are high, but, my first two requirements for a life companion are: (1) First that she love me as deeply and as sincerely as I love her. Waiting, never hurt anyone. It helps to be sure! (2) The second highest requirement has always been, is now, and always shall be, that my life's companion must, at least. Have a high school education, Even if your parents and you were to consent, I would not ask you to marry me without a high school graduation. This may sound a little harsh, but, it's my principle, never-the less!

As you said, you couldn't be unkind to your parents. You must never be unkind to them. They are the ones who made you what you are. I know your folks are grand people, like you say, and don't you worry about me feeling hard toward them, why should I?

I, too, have seen some broken hearts over the things that children did to their parents, many times over. I want your folks to like me and whatever may come of our feelings toward each other. I want your parents to approve, believe me, I want that deep down in my heart. I want them to know me before they get their opinion of me.

I've been working pretty hard for a future for the right girl. I have the things, right now, that some married people don't get in ten years and I know God has helped me. It hasn't been given to me by anyone on earth! All my friends and patrons will vouch for it. I own my own business, my home, my car, two trucks, a subdivision of 53 acres, three other lots and various pieces of equipment, and just in the past four years! I had to work night and day, and it will be some time, yet, before I stop working for a better future. This sounds like bragging, but, it is only to show how hard I will work for the right kind of a future for the happiness of my future wife and children. Their happiness is my objective. My happiness will come from that!

Shirley, I am not ashamed of what I write you. You may let anyone read my letters that you wish, because, what I write comes from deep inside.

I received your letter at 10:30 this morning and it is 3pm now. I started writing this about 1:30. I must get back to work, but I had to write you right back so you would know that I understand and that I want you to cheer up. Please don't feel bad about it all. I'll still be here. And waiting, patiently, for your letters!

I skipped over some of the things in your letter for I want to write about them later about my vacation and everything. Perhaps your next letter will bring happier news.

I really do hate to close, for I have lots more to say, but, my time is somewhat limited in the day time. Perhaps I will write more tonight, after the quarterbacks meeting. Also the second mail goes out at 4pm so I must get this, in the mail before that time. The sooner you get it, the better. Sweetheart, please remember that I think of you all the time and that my feelings for you are deep. You must know that.

I don't have any doubt about you what-so-ever. _The whole world will know how we feel some day!_

Always Yours

Sylvan

P. S. I'm still crazy about you!

Sylvan & Shirley wrote about 2 letters per week Each, over that year between Mid June 1952 and May 1953. Around 2 hundred letters total. As you can see, this book would be too long, if I were to include every letter. However, I will use some complete letters, will use excerpts from some letters and exclude some letters. I may use only a couple each month.

Shirley's next letter written on July 5 and Sylvan's last re-assuring letter written on July 7 crossed in the mail, but, things looked a little brighter for her in her last 2 letters and they were in a general note, so it will be one of the letters that l exclude from this book and will give a couple of excerpts from the last one.

"Sylvan, I was talking to mother yesterday while getting dinner. I stated that I was going to pick up the afternoon mail. I also hoped that I would hear from you and that you wouldn't be too hurt having your trip ruined. Mother said if I had said it the way she meant it, you wouldn't be. She said, I didn't mean he was not welcome in September, but, that it would be hard for me to go to school and learn anything if you were visiting at, just, that time. She said that December would the best bet for I have two weeks vacation then and wouldn't have school to worry about. All in all she was, sort of, apologizing for the things that happened that day. I am extremely sorry about your vacation in September. I know that December would be next best thing. At least it's better than waiting a whole year."

The rest of that letter was general information about what she was going to be doing in the next few days.

Sylvan was thrilled, also, that they wouldn't have to wait a whole year to see each other again. Things were definitely looking brighter all the time! Here are some excerpts from his answer to that letter...

July 8, 1952

Fort Walton, Fla.

My Dearest Shirley,

I received your fifth letter today and it made me very happy to know that you are not quite as sad as you were. I, too, was quite sad, but, I know, and, you know that nothing can stop true love, no matter what. Your last letter was so wonderful that I, almost, let a tear drop, believe it or not.

My Darling, even though it hurt you deeply, I am happy that you were sincere and straight forward to your Mother, and I am happy that you told her as soon as you got home. I wouldn't want it any other way. It shows you want to do the right thing, and, I really admire you for it, and, I'm sure your Mother does, too. It was quite sudden to your Mother, to think that her only little girl might be taken from her even before she finishes school.

Since I will not see you in September or, perhaps, not sooner than May, I'll definitely see you then, for your Graduation.

Thank you, my dearest sweet Shirley, for being my own. I'm proud that you put me first for the rest of your life. You will never regret those words. I, too, have put you first, since I first discovered I care for you.

I really do believe that God has our lives planned. It is inevitable that we should be life companions. I'll never forget that I am the only one in the world for you, because that's the way I feel about you. It couldn't be any other way!

Love you, always

Sylvan

P. S. It's no secret, that, I love you!

Sylvan received two letters from Shirley written on July 10th and the 11th in answer to his re-assuring letter about listening to, and, believing in her parents. Here are excerpts from those letters...

July 10, 1953

Neligh, Nebr.

My Dearest Sylvan,

I received your letter this noon when I got back from the dentist. I thank you with all of my heart for answering so soon and for you being you. I knew you were (are) the most wonderful person on this Earth, but now I'm positive. All I can say, is, thanks!

As you will know by the time you receive this, things are brighter. They are brighter every day. Mother is accepting the idea and knows there is nothing wrong. (This last sentence doesn't sound right, but I can't seem to say it right.) She kids me, which is her nature and while doing so she asks me things and gives me advice. I, in kidding, too, answer her and that's how things are getting straightened out. Darling, I think your standards for a life's companion is perfect. I wouldn't want them, to be, any different. I feel that, maybe some day I might show them to Mother.

It doesn't sound like bragging when you tell what material things you own. The marvelous part, is, that, you realize it has been God who has helped you. That is one thing some people forget and never should.

I just stopped for a minute to make some caramel for Larry's corn. Larry is my younger brother, who is 13. My brother, Everett, is my only other brother at home and he is 20. He has just been called into the Army and that is one reason, why, the folks are so upset. We have two Farms to work, besides livestock and Dad doesn't know what to do. He can't do much work because of his health, (He has heart trouble), and, naturally, Larry can't either, at his age.

Darling, just remember, I think of you constantly and that, as you say, "My feelings, are deep."

Always Yours,

Shirley,

P. S. I'm crazy about you, too!

Shirley's next letter was written one day later on July 11. Here are excerpts from that letter:

July 11, 1952

Neligh, Nebr.

My Dearest Sylvan

I received your letter today of July 8. Last night I answered your letter of the 7th but instead of mailing it this morning decided to wait until I answered this last letter. I wanted to do it this evening, but, have been busy helping Mother all day.

My Darling, I want you to know that your letter made me very happy this day. You said my last letter was so wonderful that you almost let a tear drop. That is exactly the way I felt when I read your letter this morning. I, like you, am very sure of my feeling I have for you. It could be nothing but true love, and I feel it deeply. Thank you for that lovely P. S.

I have no doubt about my feelings what-so-ever in my mind. I know things will work out in time.

Sylvan, Dearest, I will tell you more about Sept. when I can. I know the folks want to meet you, but we must give them time. Mother and I had a very nice talk this evening, and I find she understands things without direct words.

Yes, my Darling, I do want you to come to Neligh before next May, and, somehow I feel it will be before then.

Sylvan, I guess this is just one of my bad days. I want to say all kinds of things, but, just can't to seem to. My Darling, you at least, know that, I think more of you than I ever will anyone else.

Forever Yours,

Shirley,

P. S. I'm sure I love you, too.

Sylvan wrote Shirley a short in-between letter on July 10.

Ft. Walton, Fla.

July 10, 1952

My Dearest Shirley,

Here I am again. I wrote you Tuesday night and it's only Thursday and I just can't wait until I hear from you to write again. I just had to say hello. First thing, you know, I'll be writing every day. I really do get lonesome for your letters, believe me.

I miss you every day, tremendously, but on special occasions, more so. Boy, time sure does pass slowly when you want to see some one real bad. Some one you love. It will, really, be centuries before I see you for your graduation. I sure do hope it will be sooner than that...much sooner.

Darling, you asked me not to forget that I was the only one in the world for you...Please, sweetheart, don't you forget that my future life will not be complete without you! And the sooner that time comes, the better. Right now that seems a long time off. I can wait as long as I know your love will still be there, at the end of that wait.

As the song goes:

> "Miss you since you went away Dear.
>
> Miss you more than I can say, dear.
>
> Day time...night time, nothing I do...
>
> Helps me forget, I still love you."

Also another song:

> "Nights are long since you went away.
>
> I think about you all through the day.
>
> My buddy, my buddy, no body quite so true.
>
> Miss your voice...the touch of your hand,
>
> Just long to know, that, you understand.
>
> My Buddy, Your Buddy, misses you!"

And our song:

> Never in a million years, could there be another you.
>
> I would shed a million tears, if ever we were through.
>
> There would be no world for me, if ever we should part.
>
> Where I go your name will be right on the tip of my heart.

Only once in every lifetime, someone just like you appears.

There couldn't be another you, never in a million years!

All my Love,

Yours always,

Sylvan

P. S. I love you

Ft. Walton, Fla.

July 12, 1952

My Dearest Shirley,

I received your letter which you mailed in Norfolk on the 10ᵗʰ, today. I know you have received all my letters by now. I'm not writing this letter in answer to the one just received, only in one respect...the one about my vacation, as I want you to get it by the time you get my last one, which, also, contained something about my vacation. This will be short, but sweet. I'll write a much longer one tonight.

It is 2 o'clock Saturday, and I want this to go out in the 4 o'clock mail...it may be possible you'll get it Monday. Second, I miss you, more, every day! Third, the time passes too slowly! Fourth, my vacation will be postponed until December as you and your Mother think best.

I really had planned to come in December, as well as in September. I wasn't going to mention it until I saw you in Sept. It was to be a surprise...Now there are a few things that will be different. For instance, I'll probably have to come by train as that time of year, in and around Nebraska is hazardous for drivers, right? But, I'd come if I had to ride on horseback, believe me!

That would be the best time, for my business is quite lax in the first couple of weeks in January because of the holidays and not much business going on.

The date of arrival in Neligh will be arranged later.

We can celebrate your birthday and New Years, all, at the same time, and Christmas, too. (Of course, me being there at Christmas I would be an outsider, intruding). We can discuss that problem later. All I know, now, is that, I'll see you before next May, and, as you say, that is better than waiting a whole year.

Well, my sweet Darling, I'll close, until tonight.

Love you always,

Sylvan

P. S. I love you!

As promised, Sylvan started his next letter Saturday evening, July 12th, and finished it Sunday Evening, July 13.

July 12, 1952

Ft. Walton, Fla.

My Dearest Shirley,

Now, I'll try to answer the letter I received today. You know I wrote a short letter this afternoon in hopes that it would reach you by Monday. I know this letter will not go out until Monday, so, you will not receive it until Wednesday. I'm going to write part of it tonight and part of it Sunday (tomorrow).

I am anxious to get a letter from you, in answer to my letter of the 7th, which was the answer to your long, unhappy, letter. It did hurt me, deeply, to know that you were unhappy, because, as I said before, I can't bear to have you unhappy for even one minute. Of course, I've received 2 letters since then and I know that you're feeling much better.

My Darling, you are so sweet and understanding about everything. I could never find another like you even if I wanted to, and believe me I don't, and never will. You'll always be the only one. Please stay that way, just for me, will you, Sweetheart??? I'll try to be just like you want me to be.

My darling, I knew your Mother would understand the situation. She is wonderful to suggest, that, it would be better for me to visit all of you. O course, you and I know, that is a very long time. However, that's when it will be. That's better than waiting until next May,

60

Right? I know I will love your folks, they seem so nice. Christmas is when families get together and have fun. I don't want to be an intruder. However, I do want to be a part of the family more than anything else.

My Darling, we don't have to worry anymore about my vacation in September, do we? I'll just have a bigger and better one in December.

Yes, My Sweet, I am getting things done around the house and with you in mind. This little house will really be cute when you see it again and just for you! You can bet your life, some day it will be _our_ house. Everything I own will be _ours_ some day, From now on, to make you happy, will be my life's ambition!

Well, Sweet Darling, I will finish this tomorrow. I'm going to bed now, so I'll say Goodnight Sweetheart.

24 HOURS LATER

Well, My Dearest Shirley, after 24 hours I'm back, once again to finish this letter so that it will get to you in a hurry, so that I'll hurry an get an answer.

Sylvan wrote about working on their little house and other things in general that I omitted.

Well, My Darling, I have worked pretty hard to keep my mind, somewhat occupied, but I can't get it off of you, no matter how hard I work. It does make the time go a little faster though, and that is one of the most important things, isn't it? 5 months is a long time. 6

months have been cut to 5...isn't that swell?

Yes, My Sister Carmen is still with my folks. She will probably be there until the middle of September.

I told "Chuckie" hello for you and he said, "Good". He's really a rascal. He'll be a lady killer when he grows up, don't you think?

Well, My Sweet Darling, it's time, again, to say goodnight. I'm hoping tomorrow brings another precious letter from you.

I love you more each day, and I miss you more than I can say. Until the day I can call you mine, my dear. I'll hold you in my heart all through the year.

"Never in a million years, could there be another you."

All my love, forever,

Sylvan

P. S. I love you!

Sylvan received Shirley's next letter that was written on July 14 a couple days after he had mailed his last letter.

July 14, 1952

Neligh, Nebr.

My Dearest Sylvan

Just four weeks ago, tonight, at this time, I was sitting beside you at a show, remember? The show was Red Mountain, and consequently it is showing here in Neligh tonight. I didn't care for the show too much, but I certainly would sit threw it again if you were here to sit through it with me! Wouldn't that be fun?

I've seen several shows, since I left Florida, but there always seems to be an empty space beside me. My heart isn't empty, for you are always there, but I could enjoy going places if you were with me much more than I do.

Thinking of Movies reminds me that you wanted to know what kind of entertainment Neligh has. There is very little. We have one Movie and a Drive-in Movie that will soon be finished. We have a skating Rink, but I never skate. That's about all there is. If you have a car, but who has a car? If I go some place at night I have to make arrangements for some one to bring me home, and it sure gets complicated, for I live on a farm just out of Town.

I guess I'll change the subject, for, you will understand better when you come to Neligh.

I know, by now, you have received both of my letters and I hope to get an answer to one tomorrow. I looked hard today, but, it didn't do any good. That brings another thing up. We had better hold our letters to two a week. It will be hard, for it seems so long in between letters, when we write every couple days, but I think Father would like it better. He hasn't said anything yet, but, a little bird said he might and that would be bad! If we have the urge to write more often, we'll just stick them in the same envelope twice a week. Darling, I certainly hope you will be able to make it in December. I talked with Mother again and she is definitely set on December instead of Sept. Everett will probably leave in Sept. and that is the reason she just as soon not have company then.

My darling, I miss you very much every day. The days seem to drag when you want to see someone you love so badly.

Please, My Darling, don't worry, no matter how long we must wait, my love will still be all yours, then, as it is now. As this song goes:

You're always <u>along with me,</u>

though, we may be far apart.

You'll always be a memory

That warms the winter in my heart.

Just a small part of it, but, a very true part.-also-

I walk alone, and to tell you the truth, I am lonely,

I don't mind being lonely, because, I know you'll be lonely too.

I'll always be near you, where ever you are, each night in every prayer.

If you call, I'll hear you, no matter how far. Just close your eyes and I'll be there!

Darling, I'm still planning on sending my picture, but haven't had one taken yet. I wanted Mother to snap a picture or two before we went to church Sunday, but it seems to be that our camera doesn't work. In church is one time I feel your nearness. I felt very close to God Sunday and I am sure he will guide me!

Sylvan, tell everybody hello for me.

All my love, always

Shirley

P. S. I mean it!

Next Morning

Hello Darling! I didn't seal your letter last night so I thought that I would use this extra space to say "hello" again.

I bet you are on your way to work right now. It's just about 6:30, Right? We're always early birds around here, so it's a good thing you are too. Gosh! I just remembered I have to go to the Dentist again this morning. What an ugly Thought! Again, all my love. Guess who?

On July 15 Sylvan received Shirley's double letters that were written on July 10th & 11th.

Ft. Walton, Fla.

July 15, 1952

My Darling Shirley,

I received your precious double letter today. The letter you wrote on Thursday the 10th and the one on the 11th. Your letters are, always, very sweet. I love every word of them. The next best thing would be you talking in your own sweet voice, and speaking of talking in your own sweet voice...I'm going to give you that chance this Sunday if I get your dad's initials in time. I guess everyone knows him there, but I can get quicker connections by having his name. My darling, I must hear your voice, so, I'm going to call you at 1:30 C.S.T. on Sunday of this week. We will have a precious 6 minutes, so let's make the most of it. I hope you will be home then. As I said, I must hear your voice, dear. It will give me much more of a boost! It has been exactly one month, tonight, when I saw you last. It seems so long.

Do you think you can stand listening to my voice on the telephone?

I am so happy that Mother Baker is accepting the idea, and I am, also, happy that she understands. I knew she would be that kind of a person...kind and understanding.

I'm terribly sorry about the mess on the farm. I wish I could be there to help your Dad get in the crops and care for the livestock, however, since I can't I really and truly hope that he gets help, someway!

I'll bet that you wouldn't scare me with that tooth out, if you opened your mouth. If I could, just, see you for one minute I'd love every second of it.

I'm sure that I would get a bang out of Larry. I will, before long, too.

My sweetheart, I'm afraid that this letter will be short as I have been sick today. Sore all over, fever, headache, etc. I guess it's a touch of the flu. I can hardly hold my head up now, but I just had to write. I miss you so much. I want you so much, so, I'll write more tomorrow night, whether I feel like it or not. I sure am sorry to cut this short, but, anyway you know that I love you very much, and, that you are with me every second of the day.

I love you, always,

Sylvan

P. S. I love you, Shirley, Dear

Sylvan wrote his second letter, as promised, the evening of July 16th.

Ft. Walton, Fla.

July 16, 1952

My Dearest Shirley

Well, my dearest I am feeling much better today. I don't know what it was that I had, but it was the first time in about 14 years that I was sick enough to leave work or school for even one day. I still have some irritations from it, though. Little Mother was sick with the same thing at the same time. Carmen was sick last week with the same thing and I know several people who had it lately. Some people claim it was from watermelons we ate. Others say it was flu, however, flu usually last about a week. It had the same symptoms as flu, but I didn't take any medicine for it like you usually do. Well, that's enough of that.

I haven't even told you, yet, how much I miss you, or, how much I love you.

I'm expecting a letter from you tomorrow. Hope I get it. I do miss you more than ever, and, love you more every day. If I keep feeling the way I have lately, I may be seeing you in August. That wouldn't be so good, would it? Tell me about it, Will ya? I could be talked into it very easily! However, I'm definitely coming in December even, if, for only a week.

My Darling, don't forget the telephone call on Sunday. I'm dying to hear your voice once again. It's been so long since I heard you talk. I sure hope you still like me as much as ever...do you? I really hope it is <u>love</u>. I know I love you, because I am planning to marry you, if you will have me. As I said before, everything I do is done with you in mind. Is that alright? I mean with me it is definite, but, it takes two to make it go right. Two who love each other equally the same. Do you like me as much as I like you? If you do, then it must be love.

My Darling, I hope you are feeling much better since your dental experience.

Give my love to Mother and Father Baker and your brothers and your girl friends. Tell them I'm not as old as my age says I am. Tell them I feel about 22. No older! I probably look 42, but I don't think so. They say that, you're as old as you feel. Well I'm still a mighty young fellow yet, but, yesterday I felt like I was 100.

Well, My Dearest, Darling Shirley, it's time to say goodnight, once again. I hate to say goodnight with you so far away, but, I'll see you soon, maybe, very soon. I'll hold you in my heart until I can hold you in my arms. So darling, please wait for me. I love you, dearly!

Love always

Sylvan

P. S. I love you, My Shirley

Sylvan received a letter, today, that Shirley wrote on July 16... the same day he wrote his last letter.

July 16, 1953

Neligh, Nebr.

My Dearest Sylvan.

I received your letter of July 12, yesterday, and the one of July 13, today. I didn't answer yesterdays letter, last night, because I realized that I might receive one today, understand?

It was wonderful that you wrote a short letter and a long letter, but remember, we decided it would be best to keep our letters to 2 a week. Of course it wouldn't be hard to write one every night, right?

Sylvan, My Darling, do you know, that, every time I write...My Dearest or My Darling. I have to stop for a minute and marvel the fact, that, I have someone as sweet, wonderful and understanding as you are. I have someone to believe in and to know that they believe in you is something too wonderful for words, right?

I wonder how in the world my letters were mis-sent to Chicago.

Darling, you were wonderful about changing your plans. You make it sound so grand, that, it doesn't seem so far off. It will be extra nice to celebrate Christmas, New Years and my birthday all at once.

Yes, it would be nice if you could drive in December. It will depend on the weather, right? Let's hope for a mild winter.

My Father's name is Joe. Yes, he is widely known in these parts, as you imagined.

Well. My Darling, I will finish this tomorrow for I am beastly tired. I'm probably not even making sense. There is one last thing that will make sense...I _love you_, very much Goodnight, Sweetheart.

A few hours later!

Well, Darling, here I am, again. I meant to finish this early this morning and get it sent off, but wasn't able, for I haven't been feeling too well today. In fact, I haven't been out of bed, hardly at all. So I will write again, later in the week, when I feel better.

All my love, always

Shirley

P. S. I love you.

Sylvan and Shirley talked on the telephone last Sunday as planned and Sylvan wrote Shirley a letter right away:

Ft. Walton, Fla.

July 20, 1952

My Dearest Shirley,

It was thrilling to hear your voice once more. I sure did hate to give up the telephone after the six minutes.

I am terribly sorry that we didn't get a good connection, as I couldn't hear you, too well, and I know you

71

couldn't hear me, to well, either. Next time I call, I'll ask the operator to wait and see if we hear each other better.

Never-the-less I love you, My Darling, for being you. You are so sweet and I did enjoy talking with you very much.

What did your folks think of my calling you? Do they mind? I sure hope not, because I want to call you again, soon. I miss you so much and if I couldn't hear your voice more often, I'd probably go mad. We wouldn't want that to happen, would we? I could have talked to you for hours, My Dearest.

I went out to my subdivision property this morning to do some surveying. I learned that the County is going to put a 100'road down the South side of the subdivision. That'll really be wonderful, eh? It will make the property more valuable, especially the lots on that particular road. It will, also make the subdivision more accessible, too.

(For the readers clarification, this subdivision is called Sylvania Height Subdivision, located in the Northwest Section of Fort Walton Beach, Fla. Established in the early 1950"s before Sylvan and Shirley met.)

After I came back from the subdivision about 10am, I started working on the new little room on our house again. I did a considerable amount of work on it. It will

72

be my sleeping room. *For about a year*. I hope it won't be any longer. I don't know how I could stand it.

Well I'll quit boring you with my chatter and go on to something better. Would you mind or would you get bored if told you... *I Love You?*

So you're the one.
Well, what do you know,
And, I'm the one who wanted you so!
I don't know where you came from,
But, I'm awfully glad you're here.
Yes, you're the one I fell I love with.
Yes, you're the one, my Dear!

It's a cute little song and maybe I'll sing it for you some day.

My sweet Shirley, now that I have done some chattering of my own, it is time that I answered your sweet letter of the 14th. You are really a darling, and just wait until you're near me I'm really going to tell you what I think of you!

My dear, how could I forget sitting beside you Monday night 5 weeks ago, I loved every second of that night except the parting. I hated it (the parting). Remember the laughing we heard? And you thought it was Marcia, and after the show we found out it *was* Marcia. Boy, she can really laugh, cant she? Yes, Red Mountain was very good, and I could see it a thousand times over if you were there with me! It would be wonderful, and it'll be true someday, too, I mean you will be sitting beside me every time I go to a movie, or, wherever, we sit! You're with me in spirit now, but, you'll be with me in flesh everywhere I go before too long, isn't that right?

My Darling, isn't it wonderful how we think about each other in the same ways? We would, both, enjoy things better if we could be with each other. There are so many things we love to do just alike. There are things we both don't like. I don't care for skating, either. My Sweet Shirley, it makes me feel so happy when you say the sweet things you do, like, "your heart isn't empty for I am always there." That's just the way I want it, my Darling, and it's just the way I feel, too! Don't ever change your feeling, for I want you to always feel that after we are married for years.

My sweetheart, it is only 5 months until I see you again. It may not be too long...it's just got to go fast...it must! It will be the biggest Christmas I've ever had, just seeing the one who loves me as much as I love her. I sure hope I can drive up there. I sure am going to try. I hope it will be a mild winter in Nebraska!

Yes, Shirley Dear, if it is better that we only write 2 letters a week, then that's the way it will be. You bet your life, I understand. What ever is the best at home, that's the way it will be, because I love you and I don't

74

want to lose you. As you say, no matter what happens you'll still love me. I thank Dear God for that.

Don't worry about me being there in December because I'll be there with bells on, maybe Christmas bells.

The days do seem to drag along. Almost 5 weeks gone since I last saw you, so they are passing slowly. Yes, dear, also...

"I walk alone, and to tell you the truth, I've been lonely.

I don't mind being lonely when my heart tells me you're lonely too.

I'll always be near you, wherever you are, each night, in every prayer.

If you call I'll hear you, no matter how far.

Just close your eyes and I'll be there!"

I'm very proud to have you, Shirley, for you are so wonderful and thoughtful. It makes me very proud, also, to know that, in church, you could feel my nearness, even more. Yes, my dearest, God is with us every minute. He is helping us to acquire the real love that we'll need to live up to those marriage vows. I'll pray to God, that he'll help me to keep them. That we'll be together through thick and thin, sickness and in health, better or for worse, until death do us part!

Your picture will be welcomed, greatly, no matter when it comes, but, the sooner the better. I'm planning to take some Sunday for you.

I told everyone hello for you and they said hello, too. They were, all, sitting here when I called you today, that is, Sibyl Rose, Rose and Little Mother. Well Shirley Dear, it's time, once again, to say goodnight, so goodnight Sweetheart. I love you, miss you and want you!

I think you are the most wonderful person I've ever met!

All my love, always

Sylvan

P. S. and I mean it. I love you deeply, sincerely, affectionately and forever!

Sylvan received Shirley's 10th letter, which she wrote on July 20th, the same day Sylvan mailed his last letter. Here are some excerpts from that letter:

July 20, 1952

Neligh, Nebr.

My Dearest Sylvan,

I was so happy to hear your voice today, that I can hardly put it into words. Even though the connection was terrible, I enjoyed every second of it. There wasn't much said, but, just hearing you was enough. It will be simply grand if you do call about once a month. Jacque, Everett's girl friend, said that you usually get a better connection in the evening. Maybe we can try it at that time, in the future.

From the drift of Mother's talking, she is still counting on me going through nurses training. We'll just have to wait and see what she insists on in another year!

Won't it wonderful when we can, just, sit and talk. Phones are grand, but, you can't really say what you really want to, on them. Am I right?

Let's see, have I told you, lately, that I miss you, or, that I love you? I haven't…well, I'm telling you now! Is that alright? I sort of thought it would be.

We had my little Nephew, Mike, all day, today, and boy, am I tired. Mike is my oldest brother, Merle's, 17 month old son. My oldest Brother and his wife, Myla, have been married about 3 years.

The rest of Shirley's letter was in general. About the weather there, etc. etc.

My Dearest, Sylvan, I will close now. Just once more. I will tell you…"I love you"!

Goodnight darling,

Love you, always

Shirley

P. S. Know what, I love you!

Sylvan wrote 2 letters, next and mailed them in one envelope. 1 on July 22 and 1 on July 23, and here are excerpts from both of them:

Ft. Walton, Fla.

July 22, 1952 (Tuesday night)

My darling Shirley,

I received another one of your very precious and wonderful letters, yesterday. Each one of your letters gets more wonderful all the time. It makes me want to go to Neligh, right away, and take you into my arms and hold you and never let you go. Every day is like a week...and every week is like a month and every month seems like a year. The next year will seem like an eternity. How can we stand it any longer than a year?

My Darling, I hope I can live up to the wonderful things you say about me. You are so sweet to say the lovely things you do. I'll always be trying to live up to them and keep you happy, forever. Just keep on loving me as much as I love you and I'll always be happy! I'll love you 'til the day I die, and from then on in to Eternity! It must be God's will!

Yes, My Dear, Sweet Shirley I could write one every night, because I always think of something I want to tell you. I am going to write this, tonight, and another one tomorrow night, too, and slip then in the same envelope!

Yes, my sweet, December, this year, will be a grand and glorious month...the latter part, anyway. And, boy, will we bring the New Year in with a bang, a new year, for a new and everlasting love. We will hope and pray for a mild winter in Nebraska. It's just got to be that way…it must. Well, my sweetheart, I will close Tuesday nights letter, and I will write you again tomorrow night.

The way you have been signing your last letters is wonderful. I love you for saying what you feel. It should be that way then no one will ever be deceived. I will never deceive you, My Darling, for I love too very much.

All my love, forever

Sylvan

P. S. I love you my darling Shirley!

Ft. Walton, Fla.

July 23, 1952

Wednesday night

My Dearest Shirley,

It has been almost 36 hours since I wrote Tuesday night's letter. It's now 11:10 p.m. I just came in a few minutes ago. As you know, I went to the stock car races with Dad. There was an empty seat beside me. However, I know you were with me, just the same. Charlie was with Dad. He just got in a couple of days ago.

While I am on the subject of Charlie, we are very lucky, my darling, because Charlie wrote Marcia a letter, but,

Marcia didn't get it. She doesn't even know that he wrote her. You see, her Dad got the letter first. He didn't open it, but he put it in another envelope with a note, reading…"Get wise and leave 17 year olds alone and go with girls your own age, no correspondence, please." He, then, mailed the letter back to Charlie. Charlie said, all he wrote in that letter was thanking her for returning his glasses to him, and, what a nice time he had with her and for her not to feel too deeply toward him.

Thanks, Darling, for having understanding parents. I sure hope we don't run into that kind of opposition. Do you think we ever will?? Please answer that question! Would it make any difference? This one too!

It certainly is a long wait, in between letters! It is awfully hard waiting. I haven't heard from you in four days. It really gets lonesome. I sure hope I get a letter tomorrow!

Don't forget, my Sweet Darling, if you ever change your mind about me, please don't hold it back for fear of hurting me, for it would hurt me worse, by you holding it back, if I ever found out! Just tell me.

You can bawl me out for that last paragraph, if you want to. Maybe I shouldn't have even said anything like that.

My Dearest Darling Shirley, there'll never be another you, never in a million years! I've said it before, and,

I'll always say it and I'll always believe it. I love you so very much, that, I know down deep in my heart neither of us will ever change our feelings toward each other. I am praying to God and giving thanks for sending you to me, to be my own, forever!

All my love, eternally,

Sylvan

P. S. I love you, lovely sweet Shirley,

Sylvan received Shirley's letter written on July 23 and here are some excerpts from that letter.

July 23, 1952

Neligh, Nebr.

My Dearest Sylvan,

I received your letter, today, that you wrote Sunday, sometime after our little talk. I will write a little tonight and some tomorrow for I just wrote Monday night. If I don't hold my letters down a little, you will be tempted to answer them each time and I will receive more than two a week. I hope I don't bore you, for I sure do like to write often. (Sylvan thought, me too!)

This evening the folks and Larry are out picking chokecherries and Everett is off to see his girl, Jacque. This is the time I like to write you, when no one is around to bother me!

Sylvan, did I tell you that my eczema broke out again as soon as I left Florida. I was so in hopes that it wouldn't. Speaking of eczema, I was talking to a friend's mother last night and she was saying that they may not take me in nurses training because of my eczema. That sort of settles a question for me. I won't have to go through 3 long years of nurses training.

Shirley's eczema would plague her, all of her life.

The folks just came back, but, they didn't find any chokecherries.

I believe I will close, now, until tomorrow, for I am making too many errors.

I guess I will say one more thing, if you don't mind. I miss you, think of you, always and I love you! Goodnight sweetheart!

Next day

Well, My Darling, here I am, to bore you again. I went to the doctor, today, and much against my wishes, I must have my appendix out. More fun...Ha! In the hospital at 8am, and he'll operate at 9am. About 5 days in the hospital.

I didn't know you were a surveyor, too! How many acres do you have in your subdivision?

Darling, I'm terribly proud of you. Besides being so sweet and wonderful, you are really a man, that, any girl would be proud of. You are the kind that will always do his best to make himself, somebody!

Well, I've got some chores to do, so, I will close for now.

My Darling, Sweet Sylvan, you are the nicest person I shall ever know, and I love you very much.

All my love

Shirley

P. S. I love you.

Sylvan's letter of July 25.

Ft. Walton, Fla.

July 25, 1952

My Dearest Shirley,

I received your lovely letter, today, and boy! Was it a welcome sight when I opened the post box and saw it. The last one I received was last Monday, and that's a long wait, isn't it? "There just ain't no justice!" It sure would be nice to get one every day! No? O.k., sweetheart, just twice a week, then! I'll grin and bare it, but I won't like it. I love you, my darling, regardless of how many we write or don't write!

My Dearest Shirley, I am so very happy that you enjoyed the phone call as much as I did. I was kinda nervous, too. I will take Jacque's suggestion, and call at night, next time. "I love you so much it hurts me, and there's nothing I can do." As the song goes.

No, you hadn't told me much about your family, because you wanted to wait and see what I thought about it! Of course, I told you, that I would love to hear more about them. After you returned home, you were quite upset about how they were responding about our feelings toward each other. I do know about most of them now, though, because you have mentioned them from time to time. Roger and Joan were just married a few months ago and he is stationed at Scott Air Force Base. Everett is still at home, but, will soon enter the Army, much to the family's regret. Little Larry, your younger Brother is 13 and hasn't been called to the Army yet. I guess he has a little more time at home. You just told me about your oldest brother, Merle and his wife Myla and their little 17 month old Son Mike who is about ready to join the Air Force, or is he too young! And, of course, last, but not least, Mother and Father Baker, two of the most wonderful people in the world. Gee, I think I might have left someone out. Let me see, who could that, have been. O, now I remember who I left out...Shirley! How could I have left out the sweetest, cutest, nicest, loveliest, dearest, most wonderful girl in the world...Shirley?

Sweetheart, I am feeling much better, thank you. Yes, it was very strange that we both felt bad at the same time. It must be because of our deep love for each other.

Yes we have had snow in Northern Florida, but, very little. In 1943, in December, it covered the house tops, here! I lived in Detroit, Michigan 2 winters...1942 and 1943 and saw plenty of snow. I rather enjoyed it.

Well, my sweet Darling Shirley, I'll write again tomorrow night and Sunday night, so, I will say goodnight, Sweet Princess. I love you more than I can say, dear.

Love you forever

Sylvan

P. S. I love you, Shirley my Darling

Ft. Walton, Fla.

July 27, 1952

My Darling Shirley,

Well, here it is Sunday, again...almost six weeks since you left. Just six weeks ago, tonight we were all talking with the Heinselmans, in front of the little cottages at my Father's place in Destin...remember? What a night that was.

I was going to write a letter last night, too, but I was at the shop until 11:45. A sign man was down here from Panama City to help me get out some of my work. I had to stay, so that I could pay him. He may come here, for a while, to help out, and I wouldn't have to work such long hours. Won't that be swell?

Shirley, dear, I worked on _our_ subdivision, today. I'm trying to get some of the lots surveyed, as soon as possible, as a Realtor wants to sell them, for _us._ A while back, you ask me...how many acres do you have in the subdivision? There are 53 acres in that piece of land. (The streets in (Sylvan)ia heights Subdivision are named after you and I. There is Shirley Avenue, Elaine Avenue, Baker Street, Tilden Street and Marler Street. There is lots of work to do, yet, more surveying, street laying, brush clearing and many other things.

Well. My Dearest, I had some snapshots made, today, when I came back from lunch. I'll send them to you and you can pick out what you want.

Well, My Dear, I know this in shorter than usual, but I am getting tired. I didn't get much sleep last night. It was after midnight, before I got to bed and up early, again, this morning.

I do love you very much and I pray that God will help us, in every way, to love each other, deeply, and to help us, always, to understand each other. I always pray that God will keep you safe for me. My Darling, I know that God will bring us together when the time comes. Please forgive me for not writing so much tonight. I'll try to do better next time. Just remember that you are the only one for me, ever, and I'll always love you, deeply, and I'll strive to keep you happy, every day, every month, every year, as long as I live and on into Eternity!

Yours always

Sylvan

P. S. <u>I love you my Darling Shirley!</u>

Shirley's next letter was written July 27 from her hospital bed in the Lady of Lords hospital in Norfolk, Nebr., 35 miles east of her hometown. She was in the hospital for the Appendectomy she had talked about in one of her earlier letters.

July 27, 1952

Lord of Lords Hospital

Norfolk, Nebr.

My Dearest Sylvan

Mother brought your letters of the 22nd & 23rd, yesterday afternoon, when she came to visit. It really helped a lot, and I was extremely anxious for the visiting hours to end, so I could read them. Mother and Dad left a little early and Dad said, "The only reason was, so that I could read my letters."

This will be a terrible mess for I am lying flat and writing on my stationary.

By the time you receive this, you will know I have been operated on and I probably will be out by the time you answer. It tires me to write too much. I will, just, do a little at a time, all day long. Ok? I'm in the Lady of

Lords Catholic Hospital. I chose this hospital, because the Sisters take such wonderful care of you! We're not Catholic. Our religion is Methodist...what about you? Not that it extremely important, but it just dawned on me, that I don't know what church you go to.

Darling, I love you very much, and I can't tell you how much I miss you. I would give the world to have you with me at this time, but, I know it's impossible.

My Darling, when I was under ether, you were the only one I called for, so, that proves my love for you. Mother said something, like "She knows who doesn't love her most, anymore". Ha! In time, everyone, will understand, thoroughly!

Darling, you'll have to excuse the pencil, for it is visiting hours, Sunday afternoon, and I don't want to bother anyone for ink. None of the family came this afternoon, but I didn't expect them to. It's just too hot and too far.

Darling I do write Marcia, but it would be unwise for me to mention the fact that Charlie wrote her, and what happened. Marcia would get mad with her Dad and it would cause problems with the family. I don't want that and I know you don't either!

Sylvan Tilden Marler, you most certainly do need a huge bawling out. You know, that, my feelings will never change towards you. I love you, and, I say that with, not, a wee bit of doubt! Was that good enough? It is good to be reassured about such things, even though you are sure, isn't it?

Darling, guess what? I just sat up, alone, for the first time. That means I will be going home sooner! The doctor just came by, and, said, that, I can probably go home the day after tomorrow. By the time you receive this, I will be home.

My Darling, I will close for today, and write you when I can sit up to write so you can read it.

I love you, always

Shirley

P. S. Don't ever change, I love you as you are!

Sylvan received Shirley's letter on July 28, that, she had written on July 23, telling about her operation. He sat right down, and answered her letter.

Ft. Walton, Fla.

July 28, 1952

My Dearest Shirley,

I just sent you a letter this morning, but I just had to write, when you said, in your letter of July 23, that I just received, that, you had to have an operation. My Darling I'm terribly sorry to hear about that. I know everything will be alright, but I'm worrying about you just the same. I know, now, why I was worried last Thursday. You weren't feeling so good then. I knew in my heart, that, something was wrong. You didn't say when you would have the operation. If you have already had it, I hope you're feeling well, again. Please let me know, as soon as you can, how you are.

If you haven't had the operation, please know, that, I am with you at all times, and, that I love you, and, that everything will be alright, for, it is God's will. I know it! I seem to feel your pain so far away. I want to help share it so you won't feel it so badly.

God shall take care of you, My Darling.

I will answer your last letter tomorrow night and Wednesday night. I just had to write to let you know, that, I am with you at all times, in sickness and in health!

Mother and Father Baker and you have had your share of bad luck, haven't you? If there is anything I can do to help, please let me know!

My Dearest Sweetheart, you know that I wouldn't get bored, no matter how often you write. Please try to explain to me why we shouldn't write more often. I mean, the real reason, exactly. I like to write you, and, you like to write me, so why should anyone object?

Please, My Dear, don't misunderstand me. I'm not mad and I wouldn't get mad about such a small matter.

I was just wondering what the reason would be.

Please get well soon and remember, I'm with you, always, as I love you very much, and, I wish I could be *with you to comfort you. I know Mother and Father Baker will comfort you. Please think of me as being there holding your hand.*

All my love, always

Sylvan

P. S. I love you much more each day!

It is probably obvious to you, by now that both Sylvan and Shirley trust in a Supreme Being for their every need. Shirley attended a Methodist church in Nebraska until she was 18 years old. Sylvan attended the Grace Community Church in Ft. Walton, Fla. In his young age and had no particular religious persuasion. But, they both believed in God.

I am telling you this to warn you, in advance, that, if you are not use to this kind of thing, or, if you don't believe in God at all, you may want to put this book down, now! There will be much more to come.

Sylvan's next letter was written on July 29, 1952 and here it is:

Ft. Walton, Fla.

July 19, 1952

My Dearest Shirley,

I sure hope you are feeling much better, now.

I can't help, but worry, until I know that everything is alright, that the operation was a success. Please let me know, as soon as you can.

My Darling, you must know, by now, that you will never bore me, with your letters, or anything you do! I wish we could write more often. I wish I could see you.

I hope your eczema is getting better, too. I'll bet that is quite aggravating.

Well, my Dearest Darling, I guess I will finish this letter tomorrow night, as you say, I can't let too many letters get out too soon. So, I will say goodnight, sweet princess. I love you dearly. You are always in my heart. I'm waiting for your dearest hand in mine!

24 hours later

Well, My Darling, here I am after 24 hour lapse. I received your sweet and beautiful letter of last Sunday, when you were in the hospital. I'll finish answering your last letter, first, and then answer the one I got today.

Yes, Sweetheart, I have had a couple of years surveying. Surveying is my first love, next to sign painting. In fact, I think surveying is, really, my first love as far as work is concerned. I enjoy doing it immensely. I sure do wish you were here to help me survey our subdivision. Of course, it is possible, that, there'll still be some surveying to be done when you are here, but maybe not. We have 53 acres in that tract of land, but only about 40 will be in the subdivision. There will about 125 lots.

My Darling, I, too am glad that you didn't fall in love with anyone else, as, I need your love and ambition to keep me going. We, together, will really go places. I really do believe that down deeply. We have the very deep love that will spearhead us on to success, and success is my goal. Until I reach the peak of a successful businessman and a very good living, my hard work will not cease.

At last, Sweet Shirley, my pictures are on the way, or probably there by now. They aren't very much. Only snapshots, but there will be better pictures to come, in the future. I'll be very happy to get yours, but, please take it easy now, for a while, and don't try to do things too fast until you are completely well!

The sweet things you say in your letters really spur me on, and help me to know, that, you're really mine forever.

We only have four and one half months to wait before I will see you, My Darling. It is passing slowly, but, it is passing.

My Darling, I'm so happy, that, you're out of the hospital. I'm so happy, too, that my letters of the 22nd and 23rd really pepped you up, as I know, you must have been feeling pretty bad. It made me feel real happy when your dad said they were leaving early so you could read your letter from me. I knew they were understanding folks, and I love them for it!

Shirley, Dear, your letter was not a terrible mess, because you wrote it in bed. It was wonderful. I loved every word of it.

I'm so happy that everything in the hospital is over with. I really didn't expect to get a letter from you while you were in the hospital.

You know, Darling, it's a funny thing, I was planning to ask you what church you belonged to. Now I know. Well, I am, also, protestant, as yourself. I joined the Mack Avenue Evangelical Church in Detroit, Mich. When, I was there in the early forties. The Evangelical church name has, approximately, the same doctrines as the Methodist Church. There aren't any Evangelical churches in this vicinity. When I go to church I go to different churches. However, I'm now a Methodist. By the way, my Dad was Methodist, but he had his letter changed over to Presbyterian a couple years ago. Little Mother, Mother and Aunt Thelma have a religion of their own. Well, so much for that!

My Darling Shirley, it made me extra happy to know that I was the one you called for, while you were under the ether. That is a very wonderful thing, and, believe me, I am very proud.

Yes, My Sweet, everyone will understand, after a while, that, our love is real.

Sweetheart, I'm so happy that you bawled me out about you changing. I didn't think you ever would change, *but, I was just testing. Thanks, very much, for passing the test 100%!*

Well, my Sweet Princess, this is the end of my last sheet of stationary, so, I will have to close, for now...reminding you, that, I'll always love you no matter what may come. I love you most of all because you're you. The only one in the world for me!

All my love, always

Sylvan

P. S. There's no Human love greater than mine for you!

Sylvan received Shirley's letter, that, she wrote on Wednesday July the 31, the day after she got home from the hospital. Here are excerpts from that letter:

Wednesday

Neligh, Nebr.

My Dearest Sylvan,

Just a few moments ago I received the beautiful roses you sent. That was the sweetest thing you could have done, and, I thank you from the bottom of my heart. This is the first time, in my life, that I have ever received a dozen red roses, and I'm extremely happy, that the person I love, so deeply, sent them to me. I do love you very, very much.

I just came home from the hospital yesterday afternoon, so, I haven't been feeling too well all day. I feel much better, now, for I can lay and look at my flowers and the little card and feel so near to you.

I hope you can read this, for I'm not sitting up, much, yet, and I don't believe anyone writes, too well, on their back.

I received your letters of the 25th and the 27th, today, and was, naturally, very happy to receive them.

My Sweet Darling Sylvan, thank you so much for being so perfectly wonderful. I pray to God that I shall never lose that love, for that would be more than I could bear!

I suppose you have received my letter, that, I wrote while in the hospital, by now. I had one of the nurses airmail it for me. I don't believe I will answer your letters until later, so I can do them justice.

All my love, always

Shirley

P. S. I love you, my darling.

Sylvan received Shirley's last letter, that, she wrote on July 31, just after coming home from the hospital. Here, is his answer:

Ft. Walton, Fla.

Sunday, Aug. 3, 1952

My Darling Shirley,

I received your letter that you wrote Wednesday July 31, just after you got home from the hospital. I was very happy to hear that you are home, and, that you got my Roses, and that, you enjoyed them so much. My Dearest, they came from the bottom of my heart! It is wonderful, that, you are the one I love so much, one who deserves the best of everything! You are, without a doubt, the sweetest girl I know. I'm so proud that I have you and your love, and, that you think so much of me.

I'm so glad, that, the roses and my letters cheered you up. I hope and pray that God will, always, help me to cheer you up, when you are down. I thank God, every day for sending you to me to be my very own, and to love, Forever!

I hope you enjoyed the pictures. I'll try to have a better one made, soon.

Well, My Dear, July is finally gone, and, I'm praying, that, before another July rolls around we'll be together. I'll probably get another letter from you tomorrow, so, for now, I'll say goodnight Sweet Princess, until tomorrow, with all my love, always.

Sylvan

P. S. I love you My Darling Shirley.

Sylvan received a 12 page letter, plus another 4 page letter in the same envelope (16 pages in all) just after he mailed his last letter. I will enter excerpts from that letter.

July 31, 1952

Neligh, Nebr.

My Dearest Sylvan,

I've been laying, here, thinking of you, as I always do, and decided to write you again. Do you think you can stand it? I hope you can, for I'm going to take my time and write, write, write.

When I wrote you yesterday, thanking you for my beautiful flowers, I wasn't feeling too grand. Please excuse that messy letter. I just had to thank you, right away. It was, simply too grand of you!

Every time I look at my flowers, and that is all of the time, I know that each and every beautiful rose means you are near. I do wish you could see them, for, they are lovely!

A lapse in time

Well, My Sweet Sylvan, here I am again. I've had my supper and I stayed up late for a couple hours.

Tomorrow I get my stitches taken out, so, I should be feeling like my old self, again.

Sylvan, do you realize that tomorrow is the first day of August? Isn't that grand? December will get here yet!

Everett left on a five or six day trip, with a couple of pals, early this morning. They should be at Roger and Joan's sometime this evening. I'm real happy that he gets this little trip, for he hasn't ever had much of a chance before. He has, always, been the one who stayed home to do the work. He is the only one, so far, that's stuck to farming. Maybe Larry will, too.

Mother is playing the piano. Right now, she is playing "Memories." Will you sing it to me, please? She is, now, playing, "By the light of the Silvery Moon." Remember, we sang that one, too, on the way to Pensacola, one evening.

I believe I will close for now. (Just for tonight). I love you very much, Sylvan Dear.

Another lapse of time

Good Morning Darling,

How are you this beautiful morning? Fine I hope. I'm feeling fine, myself, thanks (I'm not crazy, just a little off).

Last night our new Drive-In Theater opened up. Just think, if you had of been here, we could have gone. That really would have been fun! Right? Golly. I really do feel peppy, today. At last! I hate being unable to do anything. I guess everybody does.

99

Did I tell you, in the letter I wrote, while I was in the hospital, that, I called for you while under ether? Doesn't that prove my love for you? A year ago, I would probably ask for Mother, but now, I am completely loved by someone and that would make it natural for me to call on you!

Maybe I had better close, for you might get bored. Nah, why should I treat you so kindly when I can make you suffer two pages more. Just kidding, of course.

Sylvan, (how I love to write that!) Did I tell you I received a lot of lovely cards? One I received from Ft. Walton. Do you know anyone there? I received lots of gifts too. Jacque, Everett's girl, gave me a nice necklace. She really is a sweet gal. (Not because she gave me the necklace, I guess it because she came from a town named after you... Tilden.) Of course, my loveliest gift came from you! Golly, everyone treated me grand. I didn't expect it from them, but, it makes me feel good. Every little card works miracles.

Good night for now, my Darling Sweet Sylvan. I love you very much. Never in a million years will there be another you! All my love,

Shirley

P. S. I love you

Shirley added a short 4 page letter and inserted in to the same envelope!

August 2, 1952

Neligh, Nebr.

My Dearest Sylvan,

I received your wonderful snapshots, and, also your wonderful long letter. Thanks a million for the pictures. I love them! Now, I can show you off!

I will try to answer the letter I got this morning, so I can get it in the mail today.

Yes, Darling, I'm feeling much better today. I am planning on staying up, practically all day, if I can.

Chokecherries are a very small, deep red cherry, consisting, mostly of pit. They grow wild, and make delicious jelly and jam. They aren't very good for just eating. Maybe there'll be some left over in December, so you can taste it.

Sylvan, please explain your Mother's, Little Mother's and your Aunts religion. I would like to know about it.

Sylvan, I am extremely happy, that, you aren't Catholic. It is hard when two people are married and do not believe the same way.

Yes, we do have a long wait until we see each other. It will, even, be a lot longer before we'll be together for good. I realize, that, it is a little harder for you, because, you are, actually, having to do the biggest share of waiting. You are ready, and, I know I can't be for a year, at least. You have waited a long time to fall in love. Comparatively, I have just started waiting.

Well, I'm closing, again. I love you, always.

Shirley

Sylvan's next letter is in answer to Shirley's last 16 page letter.

August 6, 1952

Ft. Walton, Fla.

My Darling Shirley,

No matter how long your letters are, or, how much you write I'll not get bored. I received your wonderful 16 page letter today, and, it was just a short letter, if you want to know how I feel about your writing. You could write a hundred pages, and it would still be short! I really mean it! Your letters are, always, sweet and beautiful, no matter how short, or, how long.

When I go to the post office and get the mail, and, your letter is among the bills and advertising, your sweet letter surpasses them all! I, positively, will not work another lick until I have read your letter at least 2 times.

Today, it took me a little longer than usual as I enjoyed it greatly, and I have read it several times. As I answer it, I'll be reading it again.

I am very happy, that, you enjoyed the flowers. I hope they helped cheer you up. It was awfully sweet of you to write me right away and thank me, but, you didn't have to do that, because, I know you appreciated it. They meant just what they represent, and, that is a dozen roses mean true love. That's how I feel, My Darling Shirley. I love you truly, and I'm proud of it. Yes, every beautiful rose does mean, that, I'm near to you, but, not as near as I'd like to be.

I'm writing part of this letter now, and part of it later. I'm supposed to go, with Dad, to the stock car races. I'll write more of it, when I get back.

Well, My Darling, here I am, again.

After the races, I had to go and pick up Little Mother.

You ask about my Venezuela, South American trip. You mentioned in your last letter, that I was telling a little bit about it, while I was talking to some of the folks that Sunday Evening before you left Florida, the following Tuesday Morning. It was a fishing expedition to teach the natives of Venezuela how to net fish. But, we weren't able to teach them net fishing, because, net fishing is done near the shore. The shoreline of the coast off Maracaibo, Venezuela, South America was full of jagged rocks, and it would tear the nets, so we had to teach them deep sea fishing, instead. The coast of Maracaibo is very mountainous. Houses were built right out of the side of the mountains, and you would think, that, if a person were to step out of the front door, he would fall several feet below. So much for that, on with the letter!

I was hired on as chief cook and bottle washer & food buyer. I was the only one who knew a little bit of Spanish, A _very_ little bit. A word or two here and there! We had about 16 men on the expedition. We were there 5 months. June 1948 to November 1948. After we were there about 2 months, we found out that there was a Gulf Oil Co. Camp with a Drilling rig, not too far away. We got acquainted with quite a few Americans and we were able to buy food and supplies in their commissary. We were invited to their movies, eating establishments and other activities. We found out, that, there were other American Camps in that part of South America. A couple of times we traveled by our boat to the Island of Margarita (Isla de Margarita) in Spanish. The island is several miles North East of Maracaibo.

We met quite a few American friends while we were in South America. I enjoyed my work there, but, I was happy to get back home and open up my Sign Shop again.

Well, now you know a little bit about my South American trip.

Yes, My Darling Shirley, I'll quit working until all hours of the night, after next year. We've got a few things to get straightened out, financially, before next year. My extra hard work is done because of my love for you, and our future.

I really don't like to work so hard, but, I guess, sometimes, when one has lots of ambition, one has to keep busy at something. Right?

You would have been with me last night when I lettered that truck, had you have been in Ft. Walton as my wife. As it was, I was there all by myself. I really did get tired by 11:30 p. m.

I'm happy, that, you got your stitches out and you are fast on your way to your natural self again!

Yes, My Sweet, I do realize that this is the first week of August. Today is the 6th. Isn't that wonderful?

You can never go wrong, taking a course in business for your last year. Whether you get married or work in an office, or both!

My Dear, when school does finally start, with all of the activity, time will go by a lot faster.

I'm kind of glad I won't see you next month, because, it is a long wait between now and next May, and, I'd surely want to come up there before next May.

I guess Everett will have a good time on his trip. I sure hope so.

So your Mother plays the piano, too. Of course, you already knew that my Mother, also, plays the piano. We can, all, sing some Christmas carols this Xmas.

The only one you don't know in my family is my Brother, Master Sgt. Almon W. Marler. He is stationed in Battle Creek, Michigan. He is the oldest of us kids. There are 2 boys and 2 girls.

Well. My Darling, you just closed your letter for the night. Good night, Sweetheart.

Well, good morning, you finally got up. I've been waiting for you, all night.

I, too, wish you were here to watch me paint signs.

My Darling, I would have loved to be there, with you, for the opening of the drive-in theater. Well, My Darling Shirley, it's that time again. I love you very, very much. I miss you very, very much. I'll always have you by my side.

All my love, always,

Sylvan

P. S. I love you my Dearest Shirley.

Shirley wrote Sylvan on August 3 but wasn't able to get it mailed until August 6 because no one went to the Post Office before then. Here are excerpts from that letter:

August 3, 1952

Neligh, Nebr.

My Dearest Sylvan,

I am so lonesome I hardly know what to do. All day it has been extra hard, and tonight I don't know what to do with myself. These days are very bad, aren't they? God will help us, though, I am sure. (I feel better, already. Just from knowing that you understand).

I had a feeling, that, you might have tried to call today. I found out about 1:00 today, that, our phone is not working. My heart just about stopped beating.

Jacque came down today, so she, mother and I went to the show. I was glad that they decided to go, for, I thought it might help pass the day little, it didn't! there's always an empty seat.

It really was a good show, though..."The Greatest Show on Earth". It would have been a lot more fun if you and I could have taken Chuckie to see it. Maybe you can take him when it comes to Fort Walton. I'm sure he would enjoy the things of the Circus'

I'm writing while in bed again, but, I hope you can read it. I got a little tired!

I received "Little Mothers" card and note, today, and it made me very happy. It was extremely nice of her. Tell her hello!

I will close, now, My Darling. I just wanted to let you know, I'm thinking of you. Always be as sweet and wonderful as you are.

All my love,

Shirley

P. S. I love you, my Darling, Sylvan!

The next afternoon

Hello Darling,

How are you today? I'm quite peppy myself, although, I'm stuffed up with sinus. They sprayed the town yesterday and today, hoping to avoid a little Polio, and that is probably what's bothering me. Polio is something that scares everybody, and with good reason too!

Darling, I'm sitting here looking at your pictures.

Our phone isn't fixed yet. This whole end of town is without phone service. You, really, know how wonderful they are, when you don't have the use of one for a couple of days.

December, really, seems a long way off, sometimes! Again, I will tell myself, things could be worse.

Now, I'm thinking how wonderful it will be, when we do see each other. Celebrating so many things at once, will be grand! Christmas, New Years and my Birthday. (Shirley's Birthday is January 1) I wish your birthday came in there, too. But, since it's October 17 we'll just

108

have to wait until December to celebrate it, too! I'll be thinking of you, more than ever, on that day.

I will close, now, My Dearest. Don't forget, I'm always with you. Tell Little Mother, Rose, Carmen, Chuckie, and, of course, your Mother and Father, hello for me. I love them, all, because they're part of you.

All my love, always

Shirley

P. S. I love you, very much

Sylvan's next letter is in answer to Shirley's last letter above.

August 10, 1952

Ft. Walton, Fla.

My Dearest Shirley,

I am awfully sorry that you are so lonesome. I know how you feel. I stay pretty lonesome, all the time, and wishing you were here to take that lonesome feeling away. Isn't it funny, just how, a few days, with someone, can change a person's, whole, life. Maybe next year, at this time, neither one of us will be lonesome, right?

2 long, hard, months have already passed since I last saw you.

I found a more formal picture that I had taken, a couple years back. I thought, maybe you might like to have it to scare your friends with.

I'm terribly sorry, that, I disappointed you on the call last Sunday. I thought about calling you, all day long, but I kept remembering, that, I must save for my trip in December. I will call you this coming Sunday evening around 6:30 pm. You can bet on that. That will be a month since I last called you. I figure, maybe, I'll call you, at least once a month. O. K?

Tell all the folks there, hello for me. I know I'm going to love them, all, as you said, because, they are part of you.

I pray, every night, that, your folks will like me! I pray that God will take care of all of you. I pray, that, Shirley will get well, soon, and that she'll always have my love. I thank the Lord for sending you to me to love me forever, and, for me to love you forever!

I'll bet you _were_ hurt, when you found out the phone was out of order. I know how let down you must have felt. Maybe it was just as well, that, I didn't try to call, as, I would have been crazy, wondering what was wrong.

I would love to have been with you, at the movie, "The Greatest Show on Earth". I was there in

spirit, even, if not in person!

My Darling, nothing seems to pass the time, away. Very fast, but, I am thankful, that, it is passing!

Little Mother was very happy to hear, that, you received her card, and that, it made you very happy. She says to tell you hello!

Sweetheart, I'll always try my best to stay the way you want me to. It is very difficult for anyone to keep from being different, once in a while. No matter how much a person loves someone, he is liable to do or say something, sometimes, that will hurt someone he loves. But, of course, is usually sorry he did it, later!

My Dear, I'm so happy you like my pictures. I know they are not so good, but, as long as you like them, I am happy. I hope the one I just sent you will be better for you. I wish I could be looking at one of you. I know you will send one, as soon as you can get some made.

I didn't tell you, that, Charlie went back to New Jersey. He couldn't get the work he wanted, so, he went back a week after he got here. We hated to see him go!

Carmen left, yesterday, to go back to New York. She was a little unhappy, and, I guess she was lonesome and homesick, too. We hated to see her go, too!

My Sweet Darling Princess, it is time, once again, to close the only means of talking to you, at the present time. Wednesday will catch me writing to the sweetest girl in the world, again!

All my love, always and forever

Sylvan

P. S. I love you My Princess, Shirley

Shirley's next letter was written on August 6: Here are excerpts from that letter:

August 6, 1952

Neligh, Nebr.

My Dearest Sylvan,

I received your letter, which, you wrote on Sunday, and was extremely, happy to receive it.

Yes, My Darling, I'm feeling quite well now. I'm up, and around all day long. I don't do much, except, maybe a few dishes. I would like to see my girl friends in the evenings, and maybe go to a show, but, the phone is still out. I can't call them, and they can't call me. I guess I'll survive!

Darling, I'm glad you didn't try to call last Sunday, since the phone was out. It's true, also, that once a month is enough. We really can't say what we want to say. When December comes around, we can say, to each other, what we want to say. Right? I'm afraid we'll have a hard time acting normal, but I guess people in love act a little crazy, anyway!

I'm so happy I, did fall in love so young, (As some people might say), for I feel I will be ready, when the time comes, for us to be together forever!

A lapse in time. Shirley had to go to a friend's with her Mother

Darling Sylvan, I'm back. It's wonderful to understand someone, and to be understood. I told you, in the best way I can, on paper, just what I was feeling. If other people heard me say how I felt, they would say "she's just another 17 year old kid that thinks she's in love." It's really hard to act normal, but, God will help me, always!

Darling, that letter I wrote last Sunday was really a silly, lonely letter, wasn't it? But, I was missing you so much that I had to write just as I felt. I cried that Sunday evening, I was so lonely.

Well, my Dearest Sylvan, this brings me to the close of another letter from "your Gal" in Nebraska.

All my love, always

Shirley

P. S. I love you very much.

Sylvan's answer to Shirley's last letter follows:

Ft. Walton, Fla.

August 12, 1952

My Dearest Shirley,

I received your beautiful and sweet letter yesterday (Monday). The one you wrote on the 6th then finished and mailed on the 8th.

Yes, my Sweet Darling, we'll have to wait until December for lots of things. It will be wonderful to hear you say "I love you" in your sweet voice.

My Darling, I, also, thank the Lord, that, he saved me for you. You are just the kind of person I've always wanted. Kind, understanding, sweet, lovely, charming

And, one who'll work as hard for me as I'll work for you. I know you are one who'll work hard for our happiness.

My Darling, it is hard waiting when we know, that, we were meant for each other. I'm so proud of you. It makes me so happy, that, you're doing so many things to make our future happy. I, too, am working hard toward that goal. I want to see you study and work hard, in school, to learn all you can...you'll never regret it.

It _is_ wonderful to understand someone, and to be understood.

That letter you wrote last Sunday certainly was not silly. You were lonely, as I am lonely most of the time, and, I will be until I see you again. That will be just a little over 4 months...and then, after that, I'll be lonely until we're together for life.

My lonely gal, I'm the one that should be thankful, that, I have you for my very own. You know the song..."To Each His Own." Well, I've found my own!

114

I know you miss me very much, because, I miss you more than anything.

My Dear, when you feel like crying, at any time, for anything...do so! Crying really takes a load off ones heart & mind. It relieves you of some of the pressure. When I feel like crying, (and I do sometimes)...I cry.

I'll say goodnight for now, sweetheart, I'll talk to you again tomorrow night!

24 hours later

Well, My Sweet Princess, here I am back again, after a, long, busy 24 hours. When I keep busy the time really does past faster, and it did, today. It didn't seem like I had enough time, believe me. I finished at just 6:15 tonight in time to go to the races. We just returned.

Carmen arrived in New York safely. Mother received a telegram from her.

Charlie is working for some power company in New Jersey, so he is doing alright, too!

I guess I will have to be satisfied with life like it is for another for 9 or 10 months, and then, I know there'll be some changes made, don't you? It seems like a long time off, but, it will come, eventually! God will guide us through it. Right?

My Darling do you realize it is the middle of August.

September will soon come and go. October will come and go. November will come and go and December will come and I'll go. Go to Nebraska, that is!

It's a long way to Nebraska

It's a long way to go

It's a long way to Nebraska

To see the sweetest gal I know!

It would never be too far for me to go to see you, My Sweet Princess!

Well, My Darling, it's the end of another letter from your Beau in Florida, saying, that, I love you, I miss you and I want to be with you.

Yours always and forever,

Sylvan

P. S. I love you my Darling Sweet Princess Shirley!

P. P. S. I'm crazy about you!

I will use a couple more, each, of Shirley's letters and a couple more of Sylvan's letters through August. Beginning in September, I will start using a couple of letters per month until about the middle of December. Sylvan leaves on December 15, 1952 to go to Neligh for Christmas and New Years.

Shirley's next letter, written Sunday, August 17 is next:

August 17, 1952

Neligh, Nebraska

My Dearest Sylvan,

I was very happy to hear your sweet voice this evening. It was grand to hear your voice say: "I Love You." I wanted to say it very much, but do not feel free to do so yet. I will be very glad if you decide to call again next month. I'm terribly sorry, that, you were sick today. I hope you will be feeling fine by tomorrow. I felt funny, today, and wondered if you were alright. When you didn't call right at 6:30, I worried a little more. Then when it did come through, I didn't have sense enough to ask how you were, you had to tell me.

Darling, I received your letter, written on Wednesday on Saturday. I receive a letter from you every Wednesday and every Saturday. I wish I could arrange it so you could receive my letters the same way, but it is rather hard. Someone has to go to the Post Office to get them mailed. I don't get downtown much. After I start to school the day after Labor Day, I will be able to start mailing them myself!

I went to the picture show with one of my best friends, Kathryn Hildreth, just after I talked with you this evening! Kathryn graduated last year.

My Dearest Sylvan, I received your handsome picture and I love it! It definitely won't scare anybody! They'll be jealous, because, it's a picture of someone who loves me dearly and I love him dearly!

My Darling, I love you much...much...much! I don't know what I'd ever do if I lost you! I know I won't though, for God is with us. I am forever thanking Him for giving me, you to love and to be loved by. You are the most wonderful thing that could ever happen to me! Darling, I am very, very tired, all of a sudden, so I will close. I miss you, think of you and want to be near you!

All my love, always, forever

Shirley

P. S. I love you with all of my heart & soul, my Darling Sylvan

I would like to interrupt this book, to tell you that Shirley was always plagued by her Eczema. It makes her very tired, all of a sudden, and hot natured. I will go into it, in more detail, later on, in the book.

Sylvan's next letter was, also, written on August 17.

Sunday, August 17, 1952

Ft. Walton, Fla.

My Dearest Shirley,

I'm so happy, that, my letters mean so much to you. Yours are a Godsend to me, too! I'm always thrilled at your sweet and beautiful letters. I'm, also, very thrilled, more than anything in the world, to have someone who loves me as much as I love them! Every day that brings us closer together is a happier day!

My Darling, in December, we'll do some planning for our future. It will be so wonderful to plan our future together. Our future, together, is inevitable...there is no doubt what-so-ever about it, because, I know, in my heart, that, It is God's will! I'm happy that your Mother kids you, about me. It's a good sign, that, she knows how you really feel. I hope you will hint to her, gradually, that, you are definitely planning to marry me within the next year or so. It is easier, that way, than all a once. The way we, both feel, there is really no point in waiting long after your graduation. We can talk about it, more, in December. Right?

I get kind of excited, knowing that we love each other so much, and, there being a possibility of us having to wait several years. It really would be senseless, wouldn't it?

I'll bet it was really nice to see Roger and Joan again. It's been over 2 months since you saw them.

Last Wednesday night was 21/2 months since you and I and Charlie and Marcia went to the movie. I saw you every night after that. I really did enjoy those evenings, even if they were just to sit and talk and sing.

It is only a, long, 4 months before I'll see you in person. My Darling, that'll, really be a wonderful day.

I'm very happy that Everett had a good time on his trip. It's so nice to get away from things for a little while. I certainly will be happy to get away from here for a while and get a much needed rest. I did get a little rest yesterday and today, as I was sick and felt awful yesterday. I felt a little better today. I told you, over the phone, that I am adding on to my old shop. The new addition will make working a pleasure. It will give me a shop that I'll not have to enlarge for years to come. When it is finished, I'll take some Pictures of it and send them to you. Ok?

My Darling, I love you, heart and soul, too. The things I am doing are for our future happiness.

My dear, I'll sing our song as many times as you want it sung this December, and, many other songs that we love. We can do lots of things we love to do together. When I get your picture, I'll see you every day, then. I'm so happy, that, you had some made. I'll sure be happy when I get one of you!

Well, My Sweet Darling Princess, Shirley, I, too, must kiss you good night, as it is 12 midnight, and it'll soon be morning!

All my love and kisses, always,

For now and forever,

Sylvan

P. S. I miss you more than I can say dear "Never in a million years could there be another you!"

Shirley's next letter is in answer to Sylvan's last letter, above. The following are excerpts from that letter:

August 21, 1952

Neligh, Nebr.

My Dearest Sylvan,

I received your letter Wednesday, and as always, it made me very happy.

As I mentioned, before, after school starts I will be able to get a more definite schedule for mailing my letters on certain dates. That way you'll know just when you can expect them, as I am able to do!

Yes, My Darling Sweet Sylvan, it will be wonderful, planning our future this December. I really feel we should wait until then, to say anything definite about "our" future, together. It is really hard to talk about them in our letters.

Darling, please don't worry, for Mother will realize that we will be married within a couple of years. Every one will realize as much as time passes. When they meet you in December that will be the big turning point of realization. Even my friends are accepting the fact.

Last night, Kathy Scofield, one of my best friends, stayed with me. She was looking at your pictures, and asked, if that was your car. I said, "Yes, and the house too!" She said "Oh nice, all ready and waiting, just for you!"

Darling, it sounds like your shop will really be nice. I will be happy to get some pictures, when they are ready!

Sylvan, My Darling, I love you very much, and will love you for evermore. It is so wonderful, to be loved. I never knew a person could be so happy! Mother and Larry left for Wyoming about 5:30 this morning. They took the train. They will be visiting an Aunt and Uncle there, in Cheyenne. I have, really, had a busy day, today. Besides having all the regular work to do, I had to can tomatoes & churn butter. It seems a shame. I only got seven quarts of juice out of all those tomatoes. Guess what else. I had an appointment at the hair dressers at 2:00 o'clock. Well, I finally did get it all done. It, just, took a little planning, and, I had to keep on my toes.

Darling, I hope you don't mind, but, I feel like writing. I always can write better when I'm alone. Father isn't back from the sale, yet, and Everett is off with his friend, Byron, who is visiting here from Imperial.

My wonderful Darling, I'm sitting here, writing, and, in between thoughts, looking at your picture. Oh, how I love you and your picture. I love everything you stand for. I could have never fallen in love with a more wonderful person. Sweet, kind, considerate, understanding and a million other words.

Well, my sweet Beau from Florida, I hope you have been feeling fine, today. I have felt fine and have been busier than busy, so have not been so lonely. When school starts, it will be that way. I will be busy all the time. Time will pass faster!

I guess I will give you my love and bring to close, another letter from your Gal in Nebraska. If I don't close, this letter will be too big to put into one envelope.

All my love to the Sweetest, most wonderful person on Earth.

Shirley,

P. S. I love you, my Darling.

Sylvan's answer to the above letter:

Ft. Walton, Fla.

August 24. 1952

My Darling Shirley,

Little Mother and I just returned from Pensacola, where we were since 4:00 o'clock this afternoon. It is 10:45 P. M. Phyllis, Sibyl Rose's sister, just had her baby, yesterday and Little Mother, just had to go, so I told her, that, I would take her this afternoon, after I finished most of my work. I had a pretty busy day, today. I got up at 5:45, had breakfast, went to the shop and worked until 10 A. M. I came home and worked in the yard until dinner. After dinner I worked in the yard, again, until 2:30. I came into the house, cleaned up, and by 3:30, we were on our way to Pensacola with you in the front seat, beside me!

Well, My Sweet Darling, I'll take time out to say I love you very, very much. I wish you were here and I miss you every minute of the day. Some day we'll be together forever!

My Darling, I will, definitely, be there in December, with all of my heart and soul. There aren't many things that could keep me from coming in December, if anything.

I, too, wouldn't know what I would do, if I ever lost you, I need you so much. I'll always want you near me. You'll always be my inspiration. I can, always, do things better, when you are near.

No, my Dearest, it won't be long before you are here with me. I can hardly wait until that time comes!

A little over three months and December will be here. Boy, won't that be a happy day?

Well, my Sweet Darling, I'll close for tonight, and finish it up in the morning. Goodnight, until tomorrow My Sweet Princess, Shirley. Once again, I'll say I love you.

6:30 the next morning

Well, My Darling, here I am, back again, this morning. I won't have time for my usual 8 pages, because, I want to finish, so I can get it in the 8:30 mail, so you can get it on schedule. I'm very happy, that you get my letters every Wednesday and Saturday.

It makes it very nice, in a way. If I were to miss a day it would make you worry. Right?

Well, my Sweet Darling Princess Shirley, guess I'll have to end here. It is shorter than usual, but the main thing is, that I love you very much and wish you were here with me.

All my love, always

Sylvan

P. S. I love you immensely

August 23, 1952

Neligh, Nebr.

My Dearest Sylvan,

I received your wonderful letter this morning. As always, I was extremely happy to receive it. I knew I would get a letter today and when Father went to town to get the mail, it seemed like hours before he came back. It was only about 20 minutes!

Also, with the mail, this morning I received my pictures, I had sent to be developed. I will send them, all, to you, even if they are not too good. Some could be much better. When Myla took them, she was acting so silly, she was making me laugh, wholeheartedly! You will notice, by the pictures, that, we have a nice size front yard. The big trees are Elms and several different kinds of plants. The tractor was Myla's idea. The lane and driveway, also appears in the pictures. You will get a little idea of our place from the pictures. We live just outside of the city limits.

You will see it all this December.

I love you, much, very much, My Sweet Sylvan. I really haven't, even, a little bit of doubt about that. I love you now and I will be loving you, as much, _fifty years_ from now. I will love you more, for each day we spend together will bring out traits that will make our love grow!

Darling, I really think it would be a good idea to discontinue the phone calls if the next one doesn't prove more satisfactory. It is too bad that the connections are so terrible.

My Darling, your shop is going to be another thing to be proud of. Believe be, I'm as proud as can be. You should be proud, too. Thank you for the drawings. I really have it in my mind, now!

My Darling, you just held me tight, kissed me right, and said goodnight. I loved it, and I held you just as tight, kissed you just as right, and, also said goodnight! That was grand. Let's do it once more, O. K.?

My Sweet, if you lived a little closer to me, we would be enjoying ourselves right now. The Antelope County Fair is going on, today and tomorrow. I don't believe I will go at all, unless, maybe, tomorrow afternoon. I usually am in the band, and would have to go both days and nights, but I haven't started in the band, yet. I don't believe the marching would be good for me, yet! Most of my friends are in the band, or, are working. Kathryn graduated last year, so naturally, she isn't in the band.

The rest of the family, are at the fair right now, so, I have the house all to myself. That is the reason I am writing now, instead of tomorrow. I can write better if no one is around to interrupt my thoughts!

I got my yearbook from the school, today. It isn't quite as nice as expected, nevertheless, in a few years it will mean a lot to me.

Sylvan, the funniest thing happened yesterday. When I made gravy for dinner, I forgot to turn the fire down and the gravy got too thick too quick and there wasn't anything I could do about it. I got the biggest bang out of Everett & Byron. They really had fun, making an effort, really straining, themselves, getting the gravy out of the dish. Dad would have had just as bad a time too, but he went to a sale, and I had gotten his dinner earlier.

Golly, I've got a lot of time this afternoon. I finished all of the work before dinner, so, the afternoon is free until about 6:30. Let's see, I could bake a pie for supper, or, do you think cookies or a cake sounds better? Yum-m. Well, I did bake an apple pie yesterday, so, I guess cookies would be nice to have for breakfast, tomorrow. At least, it will help pass the time. I like afternoons *like this, nothing else to do, but to write letters (a letter), and whatever else, appeals to you!*

Well Darling, I will close, now, before I run out of space. I hope you enjoy the pictures, even if they aren't too good.

All my love, for always,

Shirley

P. S, I love you Sylvan

Sylvan's next letter is in answer to Shirley's last letter in August. This will be Sylvan's last letter in August. Since all of their letters are full of the same, <u>Real True</u> **Love** and <u>respect</u> for each other, and a few side items, occasionally. There will be only one, each, for September, October, November and maybe a couple, each, in December leading up to Sylvan's trip to Neligh! This will allow room for more pages after Christmas, leading up to their marriage in June!

Ft. Walton, Fla.

August 27, 1952

My Darling Sweet Shirley,

<u>*We*</u> *just returned from the stock car races and <u>we</u> had lots of fun. You were sitting beside me! Maybe you will go, again, the next time we go.*

My Dearest I am sitting here, at home, looking at the sweetest girl in the world. I received your pictures this morning, and, every chance I've had today, I've looked at the sweetest girl in the world...my girl, all mine! I didn't know I could love you anymore than I did, but, when I received your sweet pictures, my love for you jumped 1000 notches up the ladder. What will it do when I see you in person, come December? I haven't been as thrilled in a long time as I was when I received your pictures. I've got them spread, out, all over the table looking at them, and trying to decide which one I like best, with all the different poses. It's a toss up! I'll be looking at them, constantly, until I see you in person, then I'll be looking at you constantly!

Honestly and truly, you are the kind of girl I've always wanted...your size, your cute figure, your brunette hair, your sweet face and most of all, your beautiful personality and your love for me. Your love for me is the thing I'm most proud of, as, without that love, the other things could not be as wonderful, as they are!

Well, I guess I'll answer the two wonderful letters I got this week. I received one Monday and one today, with the pictures. Both of your letters were extremely wonderful, as they always are.

My Sweetheart, it matters, little, whether you send your letters airmail or not as I love to get them, no matter, when they get here. It only takes couple days difference, but, my Princess, just keep 'em rolling, I'll still love you, just the same. Nothing can change that love!

Yes, My Sweet, <u>OUR</u> shop <u>will</u> be very nice. We just finished the floor today. Tomorrow they will start laying the blocks. I am doing some of the work, but not all of it!

I'm very happy, that, Mother and Larry went on a trip to Wyoming. I sure hope they have a wonderful time. I'm sorry Dad wouldn't go, as, I know he probably needs the rest. My dad is going to Texas on his vacation in September. It will not be before he needs it. Mother is going after Dad gets back. I don't, yet, know where she is going.

My Dear, I never mind, you, writing a long letter. You can't write one too long enough for me. I'll read it if it takes all day. Your letters are very interesting and sweet. I fall in love with you, all over again, in each letter!

My Sweet Darling, I am real happy about the subjects you are going to be taking in school this year.

Now, I will answer your second letter. Your yard looks beautiful. It really looks picturesque where you live. I sure wish I could be there, right now, but it would be, almost, impossible right now, for sure.

Yes, My Sweet Princess, we shall hold each other tight, kiss each other right and say goodnight...thousands of times, now, and for evermore!

We _would_ have a very grand time, if I could be up there now, to go to the fair with you!

We surely will have fun, looking at your yearbook and album and many other things this December!

130

I'll bet that thick gravy was good, just the same. I wish I could have had some of it.

I like pie, cookies and cake. I love the pictures. I love you. I miss you. I want you, forever, My Darling.

Good night, My Sweet Princess Shirley. I love you with all of my heart and soul.

All my love, always

Sylvan

P. S. I love my Precious Princess, Shirley

Shirley's first letter for September was about starting to school, her studies and her eczema acting up when her nerves gets out of control. Her next letter follows:

September 10, 1952

Neligh, Nebraska

Oh, My Darling Sweet Sylvan,

I was the happiest girl in Town today, in fact, I'm happier than the happiest girl in the whole wide world. I received your letter today, and, I believe it is the most wonderful one yet. I guess I always will think each letter I receive is the most wonderful one, but, it is more so today, for, it has been <u>one week</u> <u>and four days</u>, since I received your last letter. There were two letters that you mailed, that, I never received. Someone else has received some of the most wonderful material ever written. I must say, I've received the most of it!

The mystery of two letters solved!

I would like to interrupt this letter to explain why Shirley didn't receive a letter in 10 days. Two letters from Sylvan. No. one: The letter that she just received was mailed on September 4, but was addressed: Miss Shirley Baker, box 516, Ft. Walton, Fla. It came back to Sylvan a couple days later, and had to be readdressed to Neligh, Nebr. So she didn't get it until the 10th. On September the 20^{th,} Shirley wrote the following paragraph in her letter,

"You can't guess what happened yesterday. I got your letter that you mailed on September 4, and you had to re-mail it on the 6th. Yesterday morning it was quite cold. Dad came into the kitchen and asked if we knew where his gray jacket was. It had been quite sometime since he last wore it, so, he couldn't find it. Mom told him. He went and got it, and started out the door, then, suddenly stopped. He had stuck his hand in his pocket, and there were three letters. My letter from you, a letter for Everett and an invitation to a party for Larry. Dad really felt bad about it." Larry missed the party.

Your letter was in the mail box, after school, today. I was so happy to receive it, that, I could have cried the

happiest tears that have ever been. I practically ran home, so as to get to read it sooner!

Thanks a million, for the pictures. It gives me a good

idea what your shop, (opps OUR shop), looks like. Well, partner, do you think it will be a payin' proposition? So do I suh!

I love the picture of the pick-up truck, with Donald duck and the monkey painted on it. It really does look nice. The monkey is really a darling. I love him!

My Darling, that was the most beautiful prayer, anyone could ever say. It touched me deeply, for I know it came from deep inside! It was just the kind of things I try to tell God, and, and ask him in my simple way.

My darling, Sunday, in Church, I felt so close to God, and, I knew that you were well and good. Yet, all this time, I have been worrying, simply, because my mind wouldn't listen to my heart.

My Sweet Sylvan, do you know the song..."Smoke gets in your eyes." I especially like the few words..."They ask me how I knew, my true love was true? I, of course replied, something here, inside, that can not be denied." Isn't that beautiful?

Oh, My Sylvan, I am so proud of you! So proud, that, you are mine, forever and ever!

Sweet, I'm so happy, that, you have so much confidence in me. I do hope I can do as well as you think I can this year. I can tell, right now, no matter what comes up, I will be able to do it, because, you are backing me up! Every thing that has to be done has been many times easier, because, you are beside me. I have gained confidence in my self, something I've lacked, from your great love foe me! Please, always be mine.

Yes, My Sweet, I have repeated "Mrs. Sylvan Marler" many times over. I know exactly what you mean, when you say, "It sounds wonderful!"

You just told me goodnight. Goodnight to you, too, lots of x-x-x-x-s, also!

I'm so happy, that, we finally got back from Pensacola. Golly, I didn't even know Little Mother was, even, in Pensacola! Were we as tired as the last time we went together? How well, I remember that night. You were so sweet!

Don't worry I won't forget our call this Sunday. I fully agree, that, if, the connection isn't any better, we should call the calls off. We have December to look forward to. Golly, won't it be wonderful to be together again? Really too wonderful for words!

Well, my Sweet, Wonderful Sylvan, I will close for tonight. I give you all the love in my heart forever!

All my love,

Shirley

P. S. Again, I say I love you!

Ft. Walton, Fla.

September 13, 1952

My Dearest Shirley,

I can't tell you how happy I was to hear your voice today, and, how very happy I was to know that you received my last 2 letters, and, the telegram. I was beginning to worry, so that, I could hardly work. When I didn't get an answer to my wire, I wasn't sure whether you received it or not! And, then, when I didn't get a letter from you, today, boy! You should have seen me. I was really worried!

Well, My Sweet Darling, it is good to know that everything is all right!

Shirley, at anytime you don't receive a letter from me, within a couple days after it is due, on schedule, write me, immediately, because, if it is humanly possible, I'll write my letters every Wednesday and Saturday and/or Sunday nights. Like tonight, it is Saturday, but, it is possible, that, I will finish it tomorrow night and mail it Monday morning. We must not let, anything, come between us, and, nothing will. With our love as deep as it is and God's will, we'll see to that.

My Darling, I love you with all of my heart and soul, and, it will take more than human power to keep us apart, as long as you love me as much as I know you do, I have all the confidence in the world, in our love for each other!

I read in our local newspaper, "The Playground News", that there was going to be a mail delivery on Sundays to Ft. Walton. I went to the Post Office, this morning, about 9:30, looked in the box...no letter! I went to work on our building until noon. I went back to the Post Office...still, no letter! I heard some one, in the back, so I asked them, "How soon would the mail be up?" He said, "It just came in, and it wouldn't be long." I went down the street to the store, and, when I came back, I looked in the box, and there it was, all by itself. Boy! Was I a happy man! I got in the car and read it right away! It was wonderful. I enjoyed it immensely!

Yes, My Lovely Shirley, I do know the song "Smoke gets in you eyes". It is one of my favorites! I, too, have that something here, inside, that can not be denied, and, My Darling, it can not be described, either! It is hard to describe that feeling! Well, My Darling, I am and I always will be yours, forever. We'll be each others, and, we'll work, together, for a perfect life together. We'll, always, try to understand each other, and forgive shortcomings and try to work out misunderstandings, as we both know, that, there will be some. We will have to expect them, face them squarely, and, work them out! Well December is only 3 months away, now, and I can hardly wait!

Thanks for the short note, telling me that you got the telegram!

Well, My Darling Shirley, I'll close for now, telling you, that, I love you from the bottom of my heart and that, no matter what happens, you know I'll be with you, at all times.

All my love and kisses,

Always yours

Sylvan

P. S, I love you, truly, my love.

Thursday, October 9.1952

Neligh, Nebraska

My Sweet Sylvan,

Here I am, again, your stupid, thoughtless sweetheart. I am so terribly sorry for what happened. I know your love for me is strong enough, so that, I will be forgiven. Darling, every day will be a little sadder day until I hear from you, in answer to my letter of last evening. I hope I was able to make things clear!

Tomorrow is the day that our band goes to Aksorben in Omaha. (Aksorban is a week long rodeo in Omaha, Nebr. They invite several high school bands from across the state to perform at the rodeo.) We have band practice in the morning, and then, a couple of classes, and then we will leave school. I am going with a friend, Margie Spencer. She and I will be the only band members in the car. Her folks are going,

137

naturally, and a couple girls who have graduated. It will be good to see them again! We aren't leaving until after dinner. It will, probably be, my luck to forget something. We will have 8 minutes performance, but it will seem like 8 hours, when you get out, in front of the crowd.

It would be simply wonderful if you could be here, and, we could go together. The only time I would leave your side, would be during the performance! I will tell you all about it, in my letter on Saturday!

Darling, I love you deeply! More than I can say, but, I will be able to prove that fact, better, come December!

I will say goodnight, now, my dearest sweetheart. I love you much, much more than I can ever say!

A lapse of time.

Well, Darling, it's Saturday night, so here I am, writing to the most wonderful person I know!

I received your wonderful letter today, with deep pleasure. It is such a beautiful letter. I'm sorry you haven't been getting my letters on schedule. I'm sure I have been mailing them on the same days.

Our band trip turned out nicely. We won't know the rating until the middle of next week. Our band, this year, is practically a new band. Our director is new, and most of the members are new, so we can't expect a very high rating!

Next Saturday, we have a band trip to Grand Island "Harvest of Harmony". I believe that is our last trip for this season. We can settle down to, just, concert band!

My Sweet, I love you very much. How wonderful it is to say that and know you love me, just as much, in return! Honestly, you are with me night and day. I realize I made you doubt, that, these last few weeks, but, I don't intend to let you, ever, have to doubt me again. Believe me, it wasn't intentional!

Sylvan, I enjoyed going over our memories with you. Through the years, to come, there will be, many more, just for you and I!

Do you remember that Sunday evening that we met? I glanced up, just as you spoke to Mr. Hienselman. He didn't hear you, so, I let him know, that, someone spoke to him. I certainly didn't realize, that stormy evening, that, I had met the one person, whom, I would think of most for the rest of my life!

Darling, you mentioned some precious memories. The one I hold so tightly, is that you came to see me Friday night, after the fish fry. Then on Tuesday Evening, you told me you had a date that evening. It made me happy to know how honest you were, but, especially, because you wanted to see me afterwards.

Darling, you say you are sending me a gift on your birthday! That is so terribly sweet. I just hope that yours gets there on time. If it doesn't, forgive me and blame it on the darn mail. I plan on giving it four days, to get there! It isn't much, but, I think it is something you should like. It is just for you, and, only you!

Darling, I most certainly will be alone, with you, on your birthday. Maybe you don't know this, but, I'm alone with you, always. My thoughts are, so constantly, with you, that, I have to be very careful in classes. I find myself not listening, and thus, am, always called to recite, at that time!

It certainly is getting cold here, but, the winter cool feels mighty good!

I certainly do, realize, that, it is just a little over 2 months until we will be together. I count each day and wish they would go faster.

I will say good night, now, My Dearest. I'll see you in the morning. I love you, sincerely.

Sunday morning

Hello, Sylvan! I have a few minutes before Church, so, I thought I could write a few lines. O. K?

Wouldn't it be grand if you could be here to go to Church with me? I would really love that!

I forgot to tell you, that, Roger & Joan are here for 10 days, then, he will be transferred to somewhere in New Hampshire. It's nice to have them home. They won't be here in December, so, you won't be able to meet them, then! Well, it's time for church. Bye, now, sweet!

Sunday afternoon, after dinner and a movie.

Well, hello my Darling, Mother talked me into going to a movie with her. I'm a little tired, yet, and wasn't planning on going, but thought, maybe it will do me some good. The movie was "Dreamboat" and was really cute! I missed you, not being with us, as I always miss you. Oh, how I long for December. Sometimes it feels ages away!

Darling, I will close this book, for now. Do me a favor, in your next letter sing, "Memories", for me! How I recall, with deep pleasure, the songs we shared together!

All my love, always,

Shirley

P. S. I love you

Sylvan's answer to Shirley's October 9 letter
Starts next

October 9, 1952

Ft. Walton, Fla.

My Darling Sweet Shirley,

Here it is Sunday, again, and I have 3 letters and a birthday card to answer, and I am so happy to be writing you again. I'll answer the letter you wrote last Sunday, first. But, I won't to tell you, that, I have really been in suspense since you told me you were sending me a present for my birthday. All last week I wondered what it will be. Finally, Friday came, and, I said to myself..."Now I'll find out what it is." It didn't come Friday, so, I said to myself..."surely, it will come Saturday!" (That was yesterday) It did come Saturday, however, I'm still in suspense, because I opened the box, and there was a card in my box, that read..."You have a parcel too large for your box." I knew it must be my present, but, the Post Office wasn't open, so, I couldn't get it.

My Darling, please don't feel too badly because I didn't get it on my birthday! It wasn't your fault. It's the fault of the darned old mail! It's surely a strange thing about the mails...you mailed your big letter on Monday, my birthday card on Tuesday and your short letter on Tuesday, and, they, all, came on Thursday. Isn't that something? However, I didn't get your Wednesday letter until today. (Sunday) Boy, such service!

Darling, I want to tell you how very happy I was to get your big letter of Sunday, and your wonderful little note and birthday card. You are so sweet, and, I love you and thank you for everything. It's so great to have someone like you to look forward to. Again, I say I love you more than words can say! I know, that, whatever the present is, that you sent, I'll love and cherish it for the rest of my life. Darling, just remember, it's not what a person gives, it's the thought behind it, and the remembrance that counts. Thanks, again, My Sweet Darling, for those wonderful thoughts!

Thanks, too, My Sweet Shirley, for being with me, more, on my birthday than any other day. I, too, could feel your presence!

Well, now, to answer your letters of the 9th, 11th and the 12th. It was a most wonderful letter, and, very sweet of you, darling. It really was thrilling, believe me, and, I enjoyed it so much, that, I had to read it over several times, and, each time there was something wonderful and sweet!

My Darling, please don't say you are stupid and thoughtless, because, I think you are very smart and the sweetest person on this whole earth! I think, that, from the bottom of my heart! You don't have to be sorry for what happened, for, it was for the best. It gave us a jolt, and, it has shown us how much we, really care, and how much we can take from each other, and not get mad! Thank you, darling, for doing this thing!

Yes, My Darling, I promise, that, if there is something said in one of your letters, that, I don't understand, and it hurts me, I'll tell you right away, so you can straighten it out, and, I want you to do likewise! My Darling, our future love and happiness means everything to me. We must be happy and understand each other. As I said, before, there will be a lot of adjustments that will have to be made. We have to get used to the way we both live, and there will be some

143

misunderstandings. We must work those things out, and try to understand each other.

It was mighty nice of you to wish I were there so I could go to church with you, and, have Sunday dinner with you! We'll have three Sundays to go to church with you and your family in December!

I'm glad you went to a movie, and, I hope you enjoyed it very much.

My Dear Sweet Shirley, it is so wonderful of you to think about making my life happy. Just having you around, will make my life happy! I think I'll have the sweetest, most thoughtful wife in the world! Thanks, My Darling, for loving me so much! Your love, these past four Months has made my life very happy. I have much...very much, to work for!

My Darling, I wish to take this time to thank you for the sweet birthday card and the short note wishing me a happy birthday. My heart was so warm when I received that sweet note!

Now, My Darling, as you requested, I'm singing memories, out loud, as I am writing the words down:

Memories, Memories, a song of love so true.

Or' the seas of memories, I'm drifting back to you.

Childhood days... wildwood days...among the birds and bees

Oh, you left me alone but, still you're my own

In my beautiful memories!

My Darling, I, too, cherish the memories of the songs we shared together. There'll be more in December!

Oh. My dear, how I love you, from the bottom of my heart. I thank the Lord, that, he gave you to me...the sweetest girl in the world. _I love you more than ever before!_

My Dear, the letter I received from you this afternoon was very sweet and wonderful!

My Darling, I did have a very nice birthday, and it would have been super, had you been here! You will be here for my next birthday...there isn't any doubt in my mind about that. I know I'll be there for _your_ next birthday.

Well, on my birthday about 6:30 pm, I was at the shop, working on my books, when Dad called and asked me when I was coming over. I said, "Over where?" he said, "To your house." I said, "Are you there?" He said, "Yes." And added..."Aren't you going to the game?" I said, "Yes, I'll be right home!"

Mother, Little Mother, and Aunt Thelma were there. They had a wonderful vacation!

Well, we went to the game, Dad, you and me. Our team lost, 7-6 in the last quarter. When we got home, Rose and Dave (Her boy friend) were there, also. The table had presents on it and a cake. They sang, happy birthday, when we came in the door. The cake had three candles on it, for the past, present and future! Dad blew out the past. I blew out the present and you were supposed to blow out the future but, Mother said she would do it for you! Wasn't that awfully sweet? I received some very nice gifts.

My family is really anxious for us, My Darling! They, all, love you very much! If your family likes me as much as my family likes you, then, I'll really be happy. Everything will be perfect!

I'm really proud of your report card. Congratulations. Those were wonderful grades!

Darling, you said you loved to dance. So do I! Maybe there will be a place to dance in Neligh or Norfolk on New Years Eve. I'll probably arrive in Neligh around the 19th or 20th of December. (Friday or Saturday) morning!

We will dance a lot together, when we are together for good.

Your little lines with the songs were very sweet and it's just like I feel, too! "I wish you were here, for I really miss you dear, and it's been a long, long time!"

But, Darling, you know what the monkey said, when he got his tail cut off in the lawn mower? "It won't be as long as it has been!"

Well, My Darling, it's time for me to close this book, but, not without telling you I love you with all of my heart and soul. I'll never love anyone like I love you as

146

long as I live. I'm terribly proud of you. I thank God for bringing us together.

All my love, always

Sylvan

P. S. I'm all yours, forever, I love you so!

Shirley and Sylvan write their November letters, as follows:

November 12, 1952

Neligh, Nebr.

My Sweet Sylvan,

Just think, this is the 12th. Next week will be the 19th. Only 1 more month to wait. How horrible those last few weeks will be! Right now the time seems to pass slower. Well, I guess, until today I haven't felt well, for some time, and, things, naturally, seem worse. I rather enjoyed school again today. This is, actually, the first day I haven't had a headache for several weeks. The one I had yesterday sure made up for today. It was so terrific, that, I had to stay home from the last football game! We won 42-13. 5 wins and 5 losses for the season. Nice!

Darling, guess what...I found out, today, that, we go to school through the 23rd of December. That, really peeves me! I think it's rather silly to make us go to school those last three days. It will be one up-roar! Oh, well, it will be simply wonderful to come out of school, and,

147

have you waiting for me those last few days! By-the-way, we return to school the 5th of January.

I had time to stop for the mail before school, and, it was wonderful, not having to wait until after school, to get your letter!

Darling, do you realize, I haven't even told you I love you, in this letter, yet. Well, I most certainly do love you, very much.

This week and next week is my turn to spend one period working in the office at school, as an extra assignment for office practice. My meager study hall has, suddenly, disappeared.

I have, definitely, decided to take a couple of subjects less, next semester. I will, then, have time for a little rest and enjoyment! The main point is that, I will feel much better. My nerves aren't any good, and my eczema is, really, in a mess. It, really, makes my energy very low!

Let's see. I didn't tell you, that I received your letter Monday. I assume you received yours, too.

Darling, I too, wish I had been with you, at the Halloween Carnival, and, at the reception. It sounds nice! It sounds swell, that, your mother mentions me! Thank you, My Darling, for such a wonderful family, along, with, your wonderful self! I'm so happy my new family will be as grand as the one I have now!

I am planning to join the Methodist Church this Sunday. They are taking new members, I will go, and, talk to the Pastor tomorrow. I mentioned it to Kathryn. She said she was thinking of doing the same!

Well, this is all for this evening. I love you deep in my heart...now and forever!

All my love, always,

Shirley

P. S. I love only you!

Sylvan's letter of November 16th

November 16, 1952

Ft. Walton, Fla.

My Darling,

Here I am, again, Sunday evening on the 16th of November, writing to the sweetest girl in the world! Just one month from the day I plan to leave for Neligh. Darling, isn't it wonderful, when you receive this letter, it will be just 30 days from the day we'll be together again. I can hardly wait to see you, Darling! I love you, with all of my heart and soul! More than you'll ever know...more than words can tell you! I can, only show you, when I see you! As I've told you, before, you are everything I've ever wanted in a girl

Well, My Lovely sweetheart, how do you like this stationery? I picked it up, at a newsstand, downtown.

I finally gave out of paper, but, I sure do have lots of extra envelopes! Isn't it strange, how, one in love, can use so many pages, leaving several envelopes per letter. I figure I'll write, about, eight more letters, before I leave in December! You won't have to answer too many questions, in you letters, between now and then. I'll try not to ask very many, because, I know you'll have lots of work to do in school, and, at home!

When I arrive in Neligh, on the 19th or 20th I promise, I'll come by and see you, if it is not after 10pm. I don't want to disturb your family! I might, even, get in sometime during the afternoon. If I do think I can make it, in the afternoon, ill call you to find out where you'll be, when I get there. It depends on the weather. Of course!

My Darling, I still feel a little bad, because you thought I might be making fun, when I called you the other night. Please, don't ever, believe _that_, again, as, I'll never make fun of you in a serious manner, about love or you, personally. I love you too deeply to, ever, make fun of your love for me! <u>I LOVE YOU, WITH, ALL MY HEART AND SOUL!</u> I want, only you, for the rest of my life, My Sweet! True love can only be expressed from the heart! I know that, everything you have told me comes from your heart! If I didn't, do you think I would be coming, all the way, to Neligh next month? <u>YOU</u> are my whole life, now and in the future!

150

Darling, I received your sweet letter, yesterday, (Saturday), and, I was very happy, that it came on Saturday.

I'm terribly, terribly, sorry about your headaches! You've, certainly, got to quit working so hard, and, thinking so much. I didn't know you were having headaches, before! It's, probably, caused from your nerves and your eczema flaring up! Right? Darling, when we are together, for good, please don't fail to tell me, when you are feeling bad. I'll probably know, most of the time, but not, always! I would like to try to help you, if I can!

Darling, the 23rd of December is on a Tuesday. You'll have, only 2 days of school left, after I get there. Let's not let it interfere with your studies! We'll have a little time, after school is out, and also, a little time before! Boy! Doesn't it sound wonderful, just you and I together, once again? You will, probably get tired of me, before the 2 weeks are gone! Right?

How would you feel if, I told you, that, my love for you is deeper than the ocean, higher than the sky and wider than the world? Now, that's a lot of love, isn't it?

Well, here I am, at the end of the page, again. With more love for you, than ever before!

I love you very, very much, my Sweet Darling.

I'm yours, forever,

Sylvan

P. S. I, also, love only you!

Shirley wrote her next letter on November 30th:

November 30, 1952

Neligh. Nebr.

My Dearest Sylvan,

Here I am, writing to the most wonderful person, that I ever met! I am a day late, but that. Couldn't be helped!

I didn't receive your letter, yesterday, but, it was in the mail this morning. When I wrote you last Wednesday, I hadn't received your letter, but, I received it Thursday.

Yesterday, Mother and I went to Norfolk to shop, and, we stopped, on the way, to pick up Jacque. She, then, came home with us!

I wanted to write your letter last night, while Eve and Jacque were gone, but, little Mike was here, and, I had to take care of him. I wasn't feeling too well. Sort of tired, so, when Mike, finally went to sleep, I felt so tough, that, I took a pill, and was dead to the world, until this morning.

Jacque and Eve just left, so I'm, finally writing to you!

Right now, I'm thinking…tomorrow is December 1st. only 19 days.

I have two letters to answer, so sit back and relax.

Darling, I hope you can make it by noon the 19ᵗʰ. If not, I'll just have to wait another day. All that, really, matters, is that, you get here safe and sound! I feel you will, for, God is with us, always!

Sylvan, I imagine Mother and Little Mother have covered all the things you will need in this part of the country. A warm over coat, or, some sort of warm coat, overshoes, gloves and a hat or cap, if you wish! Just any number of things, along that line! A pair of sun glasses, might come in handy, because of the sun on the snow!

It was awfully sweet of your family to forget Christmas presents, because of your trip. I understand, that, you naturally, wish to get them something. Darling, please don't feel, that you need to give me an expensive gift. I most certainly, do not want that at all. I, honestly, want nothing more than _You!_ That will, always be, the only thing that matters, that I should, always have you!

Darling, it's so sweet of you to be concerned about how I feel. Please don't be worried. It has all to do with my eczema, which, in turn, is caused, mostly, from nerves. When I am through school I will be feeling much better! Next semester, I will be feeling much better, for, I will have a much lighter schedule!

My Dear, I will see what I can find out about the rates of the Nehoco Hotel.

Darling, I do wish you and I had been together at your mothers for Thanksgiving. I'm sure we would have a grand time!

Well, Dearest, Sweet, Sylvan, I have answered both of your letters, now. This letter has gone fast. I am on the last page, already!

My girl friends are having a party, this evening, but, I didn't have pep enough to get ready to go. Maybe I'm a little too lazy. No, I really, just wanted to stay home and have plenty of time to write you!

All my love, now, and always. See you in 19 days!

All my love

Shirley,

P. S. xxx next month! O.K? P. P. S. All kidding, aside, I love you, much, much, much!

Sylvan's next letter was December 6th

December 6, 1952

Ft. Walton, Fla.

My Dearest One,

Do you realize, that, in less than two weeks we will be together. The days are getting longer and longer, and, I am getting lonelier and lonelier. I want you so much, I can hardly wait to see you. I love you, My Darling, very, very much.

I received your very sweet letter on Thursday afternoon after you and I got back from Pensacola. We sort of shopped and attended to business. My Sweet Darling, I would have given anything, (within reason), if you _were_ sitting beside me, on that trip to Pensacola. It was lonesome, by my self. I had dinner with Little Mother and Aunt Thelma. Little Mother isn't coming home until Monday Evening.

I have been eating, out a little, since Little Mother left. I guess I'm too lazy to cook. I'll, probably, cook my dinner tomorrow, as, it's Sunday. I sure wish you were here to cook for me! Wouldn't that be nice? I'll bet I'd, really, enjoy it! I don't know whether I would enjoy it, or, not, for looking at you!

Boy! It's sure going to be wonderful, to see you again. You are in my every day prayers, and, I pray that our love will last forever. I thank God, for your love, and giving you to me!

Darling, the next 6 months will be like an eternity. The past 5 months have seemed like an eternity. The next will even be worse!

I have, most of the things, you suggested, except overshoes and sun glasses. I will get some overshoes. I don't wear a hat or cap or sun glasses. I prefer not to, unless, of course, you think it's vitally important!

Yes, I must give a little something to my family for Christmas. I think it is one of the musts!

Well, My Dearest, the best gift that either one of us could ever have, will be, each other! My Darling, you can't imagine how wonderful that will, be to me!

Did you know that, when, you answer this letter, you won't have to write anymore this year? If you did, I won't get it until I get back from seeing the sweetest, most considerate and the most wonderful person in the world...the future Mrs. Sylvan T. Marler. How does that sound?

Darling, I'll close for now, and, finish tomorrow night, when I get your letter. I love you, with all of my heart and soul. I'm longing to see you, and, hear your sweet voice say..."_I love you!_" that will be music to my ears! Good night, sweetheart...xxxxx's

The next day...

Well, My Sweet, here I am again...cooking dinner, and, writing on your letter, at the same time. I'm frying steak, cooking potatoes and carrots! How about having dinner with me? I sure wish you could!

I've been working on the shop all morning, and will go back this afternoon, for awhile. The glass company put the front windows in our shop, yesterday! It makes the building look pretty nice, too! I'll, probably, take a picture of it tomorrow or the next day!

I plan to go over to Destin, late this afternoon, for a while.

Darling, I received your sweet letter, today, while I was downtown. You are so sweet. I, too, am patiently waiting. It isn't very long, now...just 12 days, until, you are in my arms, and, I am holding you tight and kissing you right...right?

So, you're a brunette, eh? I thought you were a bright redhead, bright, like an apple! You know darn well, that, I knew you were a brunette...you sweet thing! I noticed a lot of things about you, and, I'll tell you about them, sometime, as if I haven't, already! Say! How about a date for Friday week? O.K. Well, how about Saturday, Sunday, Monday, Tuesday, Wednesday Thursday, and etc.

I'll be very happy to know, all of those friends of yours! Anyone who is a friend of yours is a friend of mine! I just had two new tires put on the front of the car. I've made up my mind to drive. I'll be safe, if, I take it easy, and be careful!

I'm going to close for now. All my love, now and forever! Darling, I love you.

Always yours,

Sylvan

P. S. You are all mine, forever...I love you!

Shirley's and Sylvan's last letter, each, for 1952 will begin now...

December 6, 1952

Neligh, Nebr.

My Darling,

It's after eleven on this Saturday Night, so, I'll probably, just, write a little tonight, and, finish tomorrow morning.

I received your letter, today, on schedule, but, Wednesday's letter wasn't here until yesterday. It, really did, seem a long time from your last letter, but, that can't be helped!

Merle, Myla and little Mike were here tonight, that little mike gets sweeter every day! Maybe his relation to you, huh?

Darling, I want to tell you, the weather is, simply, beautiful, here, now. Most of the snow is gone, and, it's real warm. I don't mean _real_ warm, but, it isn't cold! Sylvan, I didn't realize, that, you had a sign man working for you! I am happy the shop is coming along quite well! I hope you get all of your wishes done on it before you leave for Nebraska. Yes, I _would_ love some pictures.

That was quite a deal, about the water heater, and only 2 years old. Heavens, we've had the same one for years, with no trouble at all. You said you had it fixed, and, it stilled leaked! Sort of peeving!

Oh, My Sweet, in just 2 weeks, from tonight, we will be together. How wonderful. I can, hardly believe, December is finally here!

I'm glad you liked "The Greatest Show on Earth."

I felt that Chuckie would enjoy the circus part. Speaking of Chuckie...he was, really, cute Thanksgiving Day!

Well, this is the end of your first letter. I'm getting rather tired, My Sweet! I love you very much, My Dearest Sylvan! I, really, feel like writing more, but, my pen is running out of ink. I don't want to wake anybody, trying to find some!

I'll see you in the morning, (Two weeks, from now, that is)

I, really do, hate to close, but, goodnight, again, My Sweet!

Sunday morning

Well, hello there! I'm back again, with plenty of talk. Ok?

I certainly hope this beautiful weather continues for a couple more weeks, and, you will have no trouble with bad roads. It is, actually so beautiful, it makes me want to get out and walk for miles!

Oh, yes, I would like to go to Pensacola with you. What fun we shall have. We would, naturally, be more than willing to bring Little Mother back! Speaking of Little

Mother, I am reminded of something...I want to, at least, send your family a Christmas greeting! Please give me Rose and Dave's address. Little Mothers name. Isn't her address the same as yours? Mother and Fathers address. Carmens address.

It sounds like you, really had, a nice Thanksgiving. Our thanksgiving was great, too! Turkey, scalloped oysters, cranberries, mashed potatoes, baked beans, cheese salad, and dressing. Golly! There were cakes & pies and ice cream!

I forgot to tell you, I got 5 B's, in school, this 6 weeks. I really, was, satisfied to get a B in Office!

Well, Darling, it's getting, about, Church time, and the paper is running out.

All my love Forever and always

Shirley

P. S. I love you!

Sylvan's last letter for 1952

My Darling,

I can hardly believe it...In just 35 hours I'll be on my way to see the sweetest girl I know! I can hardly wait to get started! And, only 5 days before I'll have my wonderful sweetheart in my arms, once, again! How much I've missed you, you'll never know!

Darling, I have two letters, from you, to answer. I

Got your Sunday letter on Thursday, and, your Tuesdays letter (The one you mailed in Oakdale.) Friday! I was, really surprised, to get that letter, because, it, usually, doesn't come until Sunday!

I sure hope the weather stays beautiful, my Darling, for if it does, I'll see you the day after tomorrow, (Friday or, perhaps Saturday) when you get this letter on Wednesday, as usual.

Yes, I mentioned the sign man in a couple of my past letters, but, I presume, that, you thought I was speaking of a helper, because, in one of your letters, you said, "I'm so glad you've got a helper, now!" Well, it is a sign man. He is, really, good, and a big asset to our business. He will run the business while I am in Nebraska. Isn't that nice?

Yes, I have done all I wish to do on our shop, but, there are, still, lots of things left undone as far is business is concerned, but, I'll try to get most of it done tomorrow! Just one day to do them in. Boy! Tomorrow will, really, past fast!

Yes, My Darling, I was, very, peeved, about the water heater, but, the new one is working very nicely.

I wish I were there to get out and walk those miles, that, you were talking about. It would be lots of fun, wouldn't it? Speaking of walking…I may have to buy my over shoes after I get up there. I haven't had time to do that here! I've, really, been rushing to get the things done, that, I planned to do, before my trip.

Darling, I had the nicest day, today. Today was Christmas day at our house. Little Mother, Mother and Dad, Rose and Dave and Chuckie had Christmas and Christmas dinner at our house. They gave me all of my presents, and, I gave them all of theirs. It was, really wonderful of them. I really have a wonderful family, as you know!

You know, this Christmas, will be only the second time, that, I have been away from home at Christmas! But, in a way, I _will_ be at home for Christmas, at your home! At least, I feel that I will be, because, I know, that, your family is wonderful people too!

Here are the addresses you asked for:

Sylvan gave Shirley, all of the addresses in his family, that, she requested. I won't list them here.

Darling, I'm so very proud of your grades for your last six weeks. You are so wonderful...I love you very much! I'm going to spend this whole evening writing your letter, and, Christmas cards. I have, nearly, packed everything, and am practically ready to travel!

I, too, feel like pinching, myself, to see, if it is real!

I hope you had lots of fun at Oakdale.

I'm very sorry, that, your music department isn't what you would like for it to be! It makes it kind of hard, doesn't it?

I'll know more about the day and time I'll arrive in Neligh, when, I get somewhere around Kansas City or Omaha. Probably around noon Friday, but, I'll call you. You may be, still, in school. I want to get a room, and clean up a bit, before, I see you, because, I'll, probably be mussed up from the trip.

Yes, My Darling, I'll know you when I see you! But, definitely! How can one miss, such, a sweet smile on such sweet person!

My lovely, sweet, darling, I too, love you, and, I love to tell you, that, I love you, because it comes from the bottom of my heart. I guess we will be telling each other…"I love you!" Many times before I have to leave in January!

Well, My Sweetheart, I'll see you soon. It's just 2 days from the day you get this letter. Until then, Darling, all of my love and kisses will be riding, patiently to you!

I'll, always be yours

Lots of love and kisses,

Sylvan

P. S. I love you with all of my heart and soul!

Sylvan left Ft. Walton early on Wednesday Morning December 17, 1952. He drove west to Mobile,

Northwest through Mississippi to Memphis, Tenn. He, then, took route 61 through the Ozark Mountains reading every Burma Shave sign that he could, on the highway to Saint Louis, Mo. He spent his first night somewhere near St. Louis on highway 61. Then West on highway 40 to Booneville, Mo. where he had breakfast. He spent his second night north of Kansas City, Mo. On Friday Morning, December 19th he drove north to Omaha, Nebr. 150 miles SE of Neligh. In Omaha he took highway 275 to Norfolk. Sylvan ate lunch in Norfolk, Nebr. 35 miles east of Neligh. He arrived in Neligh about 1:30 pm, rented a room at the Nehoco Hotel, shaved and cleaned up.

He called the Bakers to let them know, that, he was in town. Shirley was out of school, and, she answered the phone. What a thrill that was! Shirley gave Sylvan directions to their farm, and, needless to say, he rushed right over to see Shirley, and to meet her folks. Shirley introduced Sylvan to her parents, and, He was cordially welcomed. Sylvan and Shirley spent Friday afternoon and evening at home. Sylvan helped Shirley with her chores. After supper, Sylvan appointed, himself chief dishwasher. After the evening chores were finished, they, all, watched television, together!

Saturday, December 20, after all the chores were finished, Sylvan & Shirley got into his car and drove around town. Sylvan learned that Neligh was the County seat of Antelope County. Shirley showed Sylvan many things, around Neligh, including Neligh High School. Sylvan learned that, Neligh had between 2,500 &

3,000 residents not (5,000) as he had assumed. Highway 275 went right through the middle of Neligh. The Joe Baker farm and ranch was, about 5 blocks from 275! I guess, that's enough history for today! Sunday morning, Mom Baker, Shirley & Sylvan went to Church at the Methodist Church. After dinner, mom took her afternoon nap as usual.

Dad lit up his cigar and watched television, and dozed. Sylvan and Shirley went for a ride and talked about their love for each other, and, about their future.

After supper, they, all, sat and watched television for a while, then, Sylvan went back to the Hotel. Sylvan drove Shirley to school, both, Monday morning, the 22nd and Tuesday Morning the 23^{rd,} and, picked her up, after school, both days!

Christmas Eve Day was spent getting the tree ready, and, placing the gifts under the tree, besides the daily chores. Christmas Eve, several relatives came over. We, all, gathered around the Piano, and, sang Christmas Carols, after which, the gifts were handed out.

Christmas Day was a wonderful day! It was one of The nicest Christmases Sylvan had in a long time! And the dinner was superb…Turkey and dressing, scalloped oysters, cranberries, mashed potatoes, baked beans, cheese salad and cakes, pies and ice cream…what a feast! Everyone was, then, ready to

take a nap! z-z-z-Z-Z. that's right!

On Christmas Day, and, the few days after, Sylvan met, almost all of Shirley's relatives, and, her girl friends. They went out for dinner or supper a few

times. On New Years Eve, Sylvan and Shirley went out for dinner and dancing in Norfolk. On New Years Day, They, all, celebrated Shirley's 18th Birthday. What a wonderful day that was, for that sweet lady!

Sylvan spent the next several days getting better acquainted with her parents, Larry, Everett and Jacque, Merle, Myla, Little Mike and with her Aunts and Uncles and Cousins and her friends.

They spent Sunday night, January 4th, just driving around town and the countryside, talking about, and, making plans for their future, together!

It snowed hard, late, Sunday night January 4th,, and early Morning, January 5, Sylvan drove Shirley, back to school. However, on the way to school, Sylvan's car got stuck in the snow, (No Chains), about a block from school, and, he had to call for help to pull him out. Not, only, did he get help, but, the Neligh News Paper sent a camera man to the scene! They took a picture of the back of the car, showing the Florida Tag, and, put it in the paper. Boy! That was hilarious, for them, in them there parts! After Sylvan let Shirley off, at school, he kissed her good by, and headed down the highway toward the East. He was on his very lonely way, back to Florida!

Sylvan drove 450 miles, and, stopped for supper, at Booneville, Mo. Around 7:45 pm Tuesday Evening he started his first letter of 1953 at that Restaurant:

En route home,

7:45 pm Jan 5, 1953

My Darling,

At the present time, I am about 150 miles West of St. Louis, in a town called Booneville, Mo. I had breakfast, here, on the way up! I have traveled about 450 miles, so far.

Dear, I thought I would write and let you know, that, I am out of the snow danger, as, there isn't any signs of having snowed here, at all! There hasn't been any snow on the ground, since I left Kansas City. The weather is fine, so far. The trip has been o.k. I, only, got out of the car twice, since I left you this morning! Darling, I'm terribly lonesome, tonight, and, I miss you very, very much. After being with you those 18 days straight...it's kind of hard not seeing you, tonight! I think of you every minute, and, it's almost unbearable! I, do, love you, with everything I have. I have just played the song..."Everything I have is yours." How true that is, My Dear. You're the only one I'll ever love!

Dear, I'll finish this later, when I get to my room. I'm going to drive another two or three hours. I'll see you later...love you very much. Say hello to the folks!

3 hours later in a Motel near Warrenton, Mo.

Here I am, again, about 50 miles West of St. Louis in a Motel near Warrenton, Mo. I just couldn't make it another mile! It is 10:45 pm now, and, I want to get up around 4:30 in the morning, so you can see, I won't get, but about, 5 1/2 hours sleep, tonight. However, I didn't get much more than that last night!

Darling, I, do, miss you very much, and, wish I were there with you.

I had a wonderful time, last night, just riding down one highway, and, then the other. It was wonderful, having you, there, beside me!

Every second we spent together, the whole time I was in Neligh was the best I have spent anywhere, in my whole life.

Well, My Darling Sweet Shirley, I'm so tired, I can hardly think! I came 600 miles since I left you this morning. Every mile is taking me farther away from you, but, every hour is bringing you closer to me. Each hour that passes means one less hour we don't have to wait, before, I see you in May. It will be wonderful to get back to Neligh! I love you heart and soul. I'm yours, always,

With all my love,

Sylvan

P. S. I love you, dear, I always will!

Shirley wrote her first letter in 1953 on the same evening, January 5

My Dearest Sylvan,

How I have missed you, this long, dreary day! I love you, so much, and have longed for you all day.

I pray, that, the days of travel will be good ones. It is, practically, a blizzard here, tonight. I do hope you missed the storm. I imagine you have, for, it didn't snow, too much, until afternoon!

Everett went after Jacque, tonight. She will be here until he leaves. She, Everett, Everett's Friend, Mom and Larry are playing Monopoly, right now. It doesn't seem right for you not being here, too!

The days will be sad, for awhile. Of course, we always miss each other, but, until we get use to not being together, all the time, they will be a bit, more sad!

My Dear Sylvan, I do love you very much, but, you know, deep inside, that, my love for you, is very deep and sincere. I know you love me!

Darling, after school, I missed you, more than ever! All this evening, has been terrible. I haven't been able to get my lessons, or, concentrate on anything! Several times I have been so sad, that, I have felt like crying, but, I don't, for, I know, that we have more to look forward to, than, most young couples! Darling:

I love you, yes I do, I love you.

If you break my heart I'll die!

Millions of hearts, have been broken,

169

Just because these words were spoken;

I love you, yes I do, I love you!

If you break my heart, I'll die,

So, be sure, it's true, when you say, I love you

It's a sin to tell a lie!

Darling, how I love to remember, these grand times we have had. All evening, I have been singing the songs, we have sung, together! Sweet:

Never in a million years could there be another you;

I would shed a million tears, if ever, we were through!

There would be no world for me if ever we should part! There couldn't be another you, never in a million years!

That's not the whole song, but, those are the very truest phrases!

I'm sorry you didn't get to wake me up this morning! Mom got me up, a little before six, to help her, a little. Please give Little Mother my love!

Darling, please take care of yourself. Promise to see a doctor, if those pains continue.

Sylvan, I love you very much. Very deeply,

All my love, All, my life,

Shirley

P. S. I do love you so much!

Sylvan's next letter was written on Wednesday, January 7th, The night he returned back to...

Ft. Walton, Fla.

Wednesday 10 am

January 7th, 1953

My Darling Shirley,

Here I am, back in the "Sunshine State." I arrived here at 2 am this morning. I drove all the way from Warrenton, Mo. Yesterday, about 800 miles! I'll tell you, more, about the trip, later! Right now, I want to tell you how, very miserable I am. I'm so miserable, I can hardly stand it, I, feel, very much, like crying!

I did cry, yesterday, some. I am terribly lonesome for you, Darling! It seems, like, I should be there, with you this morning! How can I stand being away from you the next 41/2 months, I just don't know. It, really, hurts, just to think about it! I don't know how I can come up there, again, without bringing you back with me!

I'm sure, it is God's will, that we be married, as soon as we can, after you graduate. It is, really, senseless to wait.

My Dear, I'm going to write your folks when I finish this letter, then I am going to the shop to see what has happened, since I left. Then, this afternoon, there is a funeral for one of my Dad's uncles, who died Monday night. He was my Great Uncle Charlie, so, I'll go to that at 2 pm.

My Darling, the farther I got from Neligh, the more I felt empty inside! I miss you, so, very much, that I can hardly stand it. It seemed like I should be there helping with the house, today!

I'll tell you a little about my trip. Well, I got up about 5 am, and cleaned up, dressed, and went outside, to go, and, what do you know, it was snowing pretty hard! I was about 50 miles west of St. Louis. So, I got in the car, and, drove through the snow...Boy! What fun! By the time I got to St. Louis, it was daylight. I by-passed St. Louis on the West side. There were a lot of hills, and, you should have seen the cars and trucks slipping and sliding on the side of the hills. They couldn't climb the hills. There were several wrecks. I by-passed all of the cars and trucks, and, I didn't, even, have my chains on. On a couple of hills I did slide some. Boy that was scary. The roads and streets were, really, dangerous! I, finally, got out of the snow and ice about 125 miles South of St. Louis about 10 am, at Jackson, Mo. I came, all the way home, from there, only stopping for gas, and, eating.

Well, My Darling, this is an extra letter. I'll get, back on schedule soon.

Lots of love to everyone, and, tell them I miss them, very much.

All my love, now, and always,

Yours forever

Sylvan

P. S. I love you, deeply, forever!

Sylvan wrote another, short, letter the same evening to get back on schedule...

January 7, 1953

Ft. Walton, Fla.

My Darling,

Since I wrote you, this morning, this will be, just, a short letter to get back on schedule, with my letters!

I just finished a letter to your family, which, of course, I know you will read. Everything I said comes from the heart. I love, all of your family, very much. It is, very hard, getting use to not seeing them every day!

Every minute of my stay was wonderful, as I told you personally.

Darling, I can hardly get use to the idea of not seeing you. It hurts, way down deep! I have butterflies in my stomach, and, I am very lonesome for you! I am, very happy, and yet, very unhappy. I miss you so very much, that, I can hardly stand it! I love you so very deeply!

Well, Sweetheart, I went to the shop, only for about 30 minutes before dinner, and then, didn't go back again, as, I went to the funeral, and, we spent the afternoon at Mothers. They, all, ask about you. Chuckie said…"Well, when are you going to get her, and, bring her back?" He would ask something like that! I told him, I hope to bring her back next summer! I, really do hope so, too!

Darling, Tell Merle and Myla I am going to write them in the next few days!

Tell everyone hello…Grandma, Aunt Lena, Uncle Lynn and Aunt Iva, Uncle Walter and Aunt Fay, Jacque, Larry and your girl friends.

Boy! Those days sure did fly, in a hurry!

Tell your folks, that I miss them, and that, I love them, all!

I love you with all of my heart and soul.

"Everything I have is yours!"

    (You're part of me)

        Sylvan

P. S. I love you, forever. _I'll Cherish Thee_

Shirley wrote her next letter on January 7th, also.

174

January 7, 1953

Neligh, Nebr.

My Darling Sylvan,

Here I am, on another Wednesday night, writing to the most wonderful person I shall ever know! The only one I'll ever love, with heart and soul!

It is after eleven, but, I wanted to write to you, regardless of the time!

This was Eve's and Jacque's last evening together. So many relatives dropped in, that, they couldn't get away. I should think that people would think, and, not come on his last night. It is hard enough, as it is. We shall, all, miss him, very much!

Darling, we got 2 sets of pictures, today, so, I will send them in a separate envelope. I was telling Mom, that, I wanted a full set, for my album. She said..."What did you and I, each, need a set for?" in other words, what is yours, will be mine, one day! That, really, sounds nice. Some of these pictures are, really, quite good. We showed the pictures to Mike, and, he would say..."Shirley-Sylvan bye-bye." He, most certainly is a doll!

Sylvan, I got my record, today. She had, just, ordered one, instead of two. It is, really, beautiful! How I wish you were here to listen to it, with me.

175

My Dear Sylvan, I, do, love you so very, very much! I imagine you are home this evening, and maybe, writing to me.

I, do, hope your trip was nice. Darling, how are you feeling? Please see a doctor, if you are not better.

I wrote you a letter Monday, and mailed it, Tuesday morning, so, I hope you may get it tomorrow!

Sylvan, I do hope your business was well taken care of, while you were gone, so, that, you will be able to pay off your monthly bills. I feel everything must be alright, for, the Dear Lord is certainly working with you! He has, certainly, helped us out!

Dear, about the pictures...there is one more set to come, and, I will mail them as soon as I get them.

Darling, it's, really, Wonderful, now, that, the family knows you, they mention things about you! Like how you would enjoy this, or, that, you should be here for this, or, that. They, really do, think a lot of you! I must be the luckiest girl on this earth. I have someone, wonderful, like you, to love me, and, a grand family in back of us! Sylvan, I love you so much. It is wonderful, how our love grew, in these few weeks, together! I think it will, grow, the rest of our lives!

Sylvan, I, really, loved being with you, for, those, 21/2 weeks, more than anything else, in my life. There isn't one moment, that, I could, possibly, regret those days! We, just, agreed on everything, so wonderfully!

I love you very much. Give my love to Little Mother and the rest of the family, when you see them!

All my love, for all my life,

Shirley

P. S. I love you with every bit of me!

Sylvan's answer to that letter follows.

I have wanted to mention a couple things you readers need to know, so, I will do it, now, before I write excerpts of the next letter...Sylvan and Shirley, never, drank, smoked, or cursed, all of their lives, nor did they have marital relations, before they were married, as some young people do! Now, on with the next letter...

January 10, 1953

Ft. Walton, Fla.

My Darling Shirley,

I've been home 4 full days, now, and haven't done too much at the shop, you know what I did. It rained, really hard, that day, even during the funeral, it poured! Thursday, I figured up, what bills had to be paid, that weren't paid.

The weather was bad, almost all the time I was gone, and Jim, the sign man, didn't get enough work done, to pay all the bills, however, there was, almost, enough!

It is still raining, this morning! Yesterday, today and tomorrow, I am, and, will be working on the books, and, making a new sign price list for the coming year! I have, also, made out bills to the customers, that owe us, which, ran into the hundreds. Monday, I will try to get them collected, so that, I can pay the bills! So much for the business!

Baby, I got your sweet letter yesterday, and, it cheered me up some, but, I, still, will be very lonesome, until I am with you permanently! I sure hope that won't be too long, and, I know you feel the same way! My Sweet, I love you, with everything I have...I'll never stop loving you. As I told you in person, I'm all yours! I'm just waiting for you, Darling. As I said, before, I just don't know how I can come up there, again, without bringing you back with me.

There isn't much to answer in your last letter, but, I'll go over it, and, make comments, where it is necessary.

Thanks, My Dear, for praying for me on my trip. I, also, prayed, and God was with us, all the way!

I know it's, even more lonesome, for all of you, since, Everett is gone. Tell, Mom, Dad and Larry, I love them, and miss them, very much. I wish I could have been there, so that, I, too, could have played monopoly with the crowd, that is, if you had played too! All I want, is to, have you by my side, for the rest of my life!

Did I tell you, that, when I got back to Ft. Walton, the Tringas Theatre was advertising "You For Me" for Thurs. and Friday, and, "Everything I Have Is

Yours." For Saturday! More things to add to my misery, however, I wish you could be here, we could go together. If I go, you'll be beside me, dear! I'll hold my hand, and pretend it's yours.

Yes, Darling, it is a sin to tell a lie, and, I'm positive..."It's true, when, I say I love you!"

I, too, will never forget our wonderful times together...every minute was a precious one, with you! "Never, in a Million Years, could there be another You!"

My Darling, I want to tell you something, that, I could have told you in my past letters, but, neglected to do so, as I didn't want you to get upset, and worry, too much! I know, how very much, we miss each other, and, how it hurts, so, I didn't want to add the awful misery, that, I have suffered, to yours to! Well, on Monday night, after traveling 600 miles, I stopped at a motel to spend the night, as you know. That's when I wrote you the first letter. I went to bed, about 11:30 pm. And. Got up about 4:45 am. I went to the bathroom to clean-up. I took off my ring to wash my hands. I got all my belongings together, went out to the car, and, as I told you before, it was snowing very hard! , so, I put my gloves on and drove off. It was very cold, in the car, until the heater came on, about 150 miles south. I pulled my gloves off. My ring (your ring) wasn't on my finger, and, at that very moment, I remembered, I had left it in the bath room, at the Motel. Oh, My Dear, how miserable I was!

It was like leaving you there! I. actually, cried for 2 hours, and, I mean really cried! I thought of going back, but, I, also, thought of the dangerous, icy, roads. The only thing I knew to do was pray to God, that I would get it back! I prayed as I cried, and, asking Him to let the lady send it! I didn't, even, remember the name of the motel, so I couldn't call them!

Well, My Sweet Darling, Shirley, my prayers were answered. Yesterday, I got a card, reading, as follows: "In cleaning room no. 3, this morning, a class ring was found. If it belongs to you, please notify us.

"Lin-Wal Motel, Wright City, Mo. I, immediately, wired them to...send it insured. How, I did thank, and, still do thank God, for being so wonderful to me!

My Darling, we do, have so many things to thank God for. I know, that God will be with us, the rest of our lives, because, we believe so deeply!

Well, My Sweet, I expect your letter, tomorrow (Sunday) as it didn't come today, so, I'll answer the rest of this letter then. I'll say good night, My Sweet Princess, until we are together tomorrow night! I, do, love you so...Good night, Darling!

36 hours later

Well, my wonderful Sweet Darling, I'm back, again, to finish your letter. Little Mother and I have been over to Destin since 2 pm this afternoon, and it's 9 pm now.

I received your letter, and, it was so very sweet and wonderful! I loved every sweet line in it. Darling, I love you with all my heart and soul! I'll answer that letter before I close.

Darling, I, also, received the wonderful pictures, today. I sure do like every one of them. I can't tell you how much they mean to me! Yes, My Darling, what do we need with 2 sets of them for, after all, you will, probably, be here in June, anyway, and, everything I have is yours!

It looks like I won't get to see that picture show, after all, as I am going to the quarterback club meeting tomorrow night!

My Dear, I've got my set of pictures back, too, and, I'll send them, right away. Some of them are not very good, though, but, they are all yours, just the same.

It was awfully sweet of Mike to look and ask for me! I miss him, too, and his sweet "awite."

It was terribly sweet for Mom, to think of us as being one some day. Maybe, as soon as you graduate! I'm so happy that your family speaks of me some. Please tell me some of the things they say, once in a while. I sure do miss them, very much!

Darling, I was thinking, a week ago, last night, we were at the Granada Theater seeing "You For Me." And, last Sunday night, we were riding the highways, talking and singing! How I wish I were there, with you, tonight!

Well, it's only 124 days until the May 15th, when I will see you, again…Oh, happy day!

I showed, all of your pictures, to my family, and, they liked them, very much. They said, you certainly have a nice looking family, and that, your Mother looked very sweet! Naturally, they said…you were a very sweet girl, and that, you really, looked happy, in your pictures, with me! I'm very proud of your pictures with me!

Darling, remember, that, I love you and miss you, and, want you close to me, as soon as possible, just as you want me, the same way!

I'm yours and only yours, for all my life and forever!

Sylvan

P. S. I love you with all that I have!

Shirley's reply

January 14, 1953

Neligh, Nebr.

My Darling Sylvan,

I received your letter, today! It has, really, only been four days, since your last one, but, it has seemed like weeks.

Darling I, do, love your letters. They mean so much to me. Sylvan, I love you…I would say, that, is the reason I love your letters! Every letter is so sweet, and, means so much! They do help, but, I'm still not satisfied. I pray for the day we will be together!

Darling, I'm sorry about the weather, and that, Jim wasn't able to make enough, so that, you could pay the bills. I've been wondering about it, every since you left. You spent too much on me, while you were here. Yes, My Dear, I understand why! But, still I feel you did! But, darling, I did appreciate everything!

Yes, My Darling, I do know how lonesome and miserable you have been!

My Dearest Sylvan, right now, I want you to know, that, I could tell, by the letter I received, Saturday, that, you had something more, to be miserable about, than I knew about. I, also, knew, that, you would tell me about it, when it was time! Believe me, I know, just, how you felt, because, I've said, before, that, If I ever lost my ring, I would never forgive myself, and, certainly wouldn't know what to do. Oh, My Darling, God is with us all the time. We can never fail, with, our sincere belief! I love you very much! We would have loved seeing..."Everything I have is yours." I am sure! We shall, always, love everything, we do, together. Work and play! Work, will be play...when it is with and for you!

Darling, I, too, can sincerely say..."Everything I have is yours!", for you are, certainly, part of me!

Darling, we will try for the last part of May, or, the first of June. I know the family is behind us. Mother, quite frequently, will say something to that effect!

We got a letter from Roger, today, and, he commented on your visit here! Mother or some of the rest of the family, probably, had written him about you. He said..."It seems to me, that, everyone approves of the fellow!" He said a little more, but, I only got to glance at the letter, so, I can't recall, what else.

Yes, Sylvan, _it is,_ quite lonesome, around here, without Everett. We have received several letters from him, but, we can't write him, for, he will be re-stationed soon. Jacque is, certainly, lost without Eve, and, he without her!

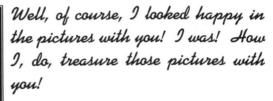

Well, of course, I looked happy in the pictures with you! I was! How I, do, treasure those pictures with you!

Are you quite sure the 15th will be, when you will see me? School is out the 22nd. The last week seniors will not have to go to school. The Sunday before that, will be the Bac. Service. I want you to be here for that! I'm not sure of the date of the graduation.

Darling, please tell your family hello for me! I do love them, already, without knowing them too well. You could tell Jim hello, for I feel like I must know him.

My Dear, just remember, that, I love you, want you and miss you all the time!

All my love, for all my life

I'm yours

Shirley

P. S. I love you with all of me

P. P. S. I do hope you have been able to read this. I'm tired and pep-less tonight!

P. P. S. hey! I forgot to tell you, that, Grandmother, certainly, thought you wrote a nice letter!

Sylvan's last letter for January 1953

January 17, 1953

Ft. Walton, Fla.

My Darling Sweet Shirley,

Two weeks have passed since we were together in Norfolk, and, as you said, it seems like centuries. I do miss you, very, very much, and, I love you so much it hurts way down deep. My Dear, it's just, 118 days, now, until I leave here, again, to see the most wonderful girl in all, the world! Just 4 months. 2 less weeks to wait, isn't that wonderful? Just 17 weeks until we are in each others arms, and, maybe, permanently. I sure am Praying, that, it will be possible!

Darling, I received your ring Thursday, and, I sure was a happy man! It was like having you here with

185

me! I did miss it terribly much, but, I can't say, in words, how very much I miss you, My Sweet Shirley!

Dearest, I received your sweet note, and the pictures. I am crazy about, all of, them. They are, really, wonderful! Oh, My Darling, how I, do, miss, everyone, and, I do love them, all, just as if they were my own folks!

I am so happy, that, your Mother liked the letter I wrote. It was sweet of her to say what she did. I hope I can, always, be that kind of a person, and, live up to those nice comments! I am very proud of your family's friendship and love, for, I feel, they are very true and sincere, just like you, My Darling!

I am getting back into the grove of working again, for a change. It has been a little difficult, getting back into the grind. I worked until 9:30, tonight, building signs, and, coating out boards...getting them ready for Jim. Tuesday the orders started coming in, and, we have been pretty rushed, all week! I don't mind, at all, for, it keeps me busy, for one thing, and, I need the money, for another!

Well, My Darling, I'll say goodnight, with much love and kisses, until tomorrow night! I love you, with, all of my heart and soul..."I'm Yours", "Everything I have is yours", "You for me", "Never in a million years", It's a sin to tell a lie", "Be sure it's true", You and I ", "Because" I'll always love you, and, you'll have all of my love for all of my life! Good night, My Sweet precious Princess...I do love you so!

24 hours latter

My Darling, I'm back again, and, I have missed you, very much, since last night! I've been very lonesome for you, and, even more so this afternoon, as, I didn't get your Wednesday letter today. I was very disappointed! I went back to the post office, again early this afternoon...no letter...later this afternoon...nope! Maybe I'll get it tomorrow, for sure!

Darling, before I come up in May, I might have our car painted, if it is alright with you. I'm not sure I can afford it. If I do, what color would you like it to be? I want you to have the color you like!

Well, My Sweetheart, I'll say goodnight for tonight. Please give all my love to all the folks, and, Eve, when you write him. I love you very, very much, and, it hurts so, not to be near you, so I can just touch you!

Goodnight, My Darling I'm all yours forever

Sylvan

P. S. I'll never love anyone but YOU!

Shirley's last letter in January 1953

January 26, 1953

Neligh, Nebr.

My Darling Sylvan,

I received your letter, per usual. I am always so happy to get your letter, and, always look forward to the next one!

Sylvan, I am, always, very lonesome, for you, every day, <u>too</u>!

I'm sorry you didn't get my letter until late, but, it was the storm.

Darling your letter was very sweet and wonderful!

I'm so happy you think I am so good in so many ways. I will try to live up to your expectations, always. I, do, love you, so much. You are, most certainly, the most wonderful person I shall ever know. The only one I shall ever love with all of my heart and soul, forever! I am, really, the luckiest one!

You asked me where I wanted to go, for a couple days, after we are married. I say...I want to go where you go, Darling! It doesn't matter.

Well, I'm glad you did get your Wednesday letter on Wednesday.

Mother is feeling much better. She has been painting and cleaning the boy's room, the last two days. I don't think she should, yet, but she is! Once she said..."I *want to get it fixed, so, I won't be ashamed to ask somebody to stay with us! She said she wasn't going to let you stay in a hotel, the next time you come!"*

Mom said a couple things, this morning, that stood out...I had been busy, all morning, and, about noon, I was a little tired and nervous. She made the statement, that, she didn't think I could take an office job, unless I got better, all of a sudden! Then, at dinner Larry was talking to me about taking over a job for him this summer. I said, I couldn't, because I won't be around this summer. Then, Mom said something, like, "She will, probably, be married by then!" Larry said..."Poor Sylvan, I think I'll write and warn him what he's getting!" Jokingly, of course! I felt, that, there was meaning in Mothers words!

Darling, it's grand, that you sold a sign for my rings. Yes, you, certainly, better want to get them here in May!

Sylvan sold and installed a 10' x 20' highway billboard on North Eglin Parkway (Highway 85), between the bridges, for Vandegriff Jewelers for Shirley's engagement and wedding rings in early 1953, worth several hundred dollars!

We had French fried onions for dinner, and, I remembered the last time I ate them. We had them the last Saturday night in Norfolk, remember? I know you do!

Sylvan, tell all the folks, that, I send them my love.

Darling, I love you so much. Everything I have is yours. You're a part of me. How true that song is. I heard it this morning, just after, I read your letter. It seemed so appropriate.

Darling, I finally received my grades...4 B's and 1 A. I guess that isn't too bad.

Darling, can you, really, make out my writing? I, sometimes, wonder! I get to thinking so fast, that, I write worse than usual. I have, always, wanted to be a pretty writer, but, I can't seem to accomplish that!

Darling, this letter has, certainly, gone fast, but, I guess I have said about everything. I'll, always love you!

All my love, for all my life,

Shirley

P. S. I love you so much, my heart aches for you!

Sylvan's first February letter

February 4, 1953

Ft. Walton, Fla.

I received your sweet letter, today, with much happiness, as usual! I sure wish I could receive you instead of your letters. It would be much nicer to talk to you. There are so many things we could talk about!

Darling, I love you so very much, and that, you love me, is, all that matters, and, our future life together. I wish I could say the things, that, I want to say to you, personally, instead of writing them!

Darling it wouldn't be hard to plan our wedding before you graduate, if Mom and Dad give their consent. We could plan it for, around, the first part of June. We will see! I, really, think Mom and Dad know it's going to be, but, when?

I haven't decided whether or not, I should stay at your house. I, naturally, would love to. It's an honor to be liked by your family, enough, for them to ask me. I sure do love them. They are so wonderful!

Yes, My Darling, I'm looking forward to the time we can be one, to keep, for the rest of my life, as my one and only love, to whom I'll cherish with heart and soul. The only person I can really trust to the fullest extent! The sweetest person I know, and, one who'll love me as much as I love her!

Yes, dear, our marriage will be a little hard for you and your parents to get use to not being around each other, for the first year. After that, everyone will be a lot happier, and, it will smooth out! Darling, believe me...I do love Mom and Dad, and, I, too, will be a little hurt, 'cause, I know they will be feeling lonesome for you, and, you for them!

I'm very happy, that, Mom took you to see a doctor & that, he helped you some. I sure hope you will feel better. I know you will, for, God is surely with us both! So far, God has helped us all the way. I know our Prayers and thanks to Him, has done a world of good!

It was nice that Kathryn stayed with you. I'm glad you went to a show. I wish I could have been with you, too! I do miss our going out, together, but, we will have a whole life time of going out together, though! Right?

All the folks, here, say to tell you hello, and send their love.

I'm very sorry, that, Mike was sick, again. I sure hope he is well, now!

I'm looking forward to that, extra, letter you said you would write!

Darling, I am thinking of you, constantly, and, all of the wonderful times we will have together, and, how wonderful our life will be together! Everything we do will be for each other!

Give my love to all of the folks!

I love you, with, all or my heart and soul. All my love, for all my life!

Sylvan

P. S. I'm yours always…everything I have is yours!

Shirley's first letter in February:

Saturday, February 7, 1953

Neligh, Nebr.

My Dearest Sylvan,

I received your letter, this morning, with much happiness! As you said...it would be much nicer to receive you instead. We, certainly, wouldn't have a hard time, finding something to talk about! Am I right?

Yes, My Darling, just as soon as Mom has giving her consent, we can start planning things, definitely! I do know, that, we will, feel much better, when things are settled, Darling! I want you to know, that, I definitely, want to marry you, soon after my graduation!

My dearest, I just can't think of a color to paint our car! Nothing sets in my mind, except, the color it is now! You and I and that car have been, everywhere together, and, I feel sort of sentimental about it! Whatever you choose, is fine with me!

Merle, Myla and Mike were in, tonight, for the first time in several weeks. Mike is busy sleeping, right now!

My Darling, every single day, I am thinking of you. I am, always, thinking of the things we will do, together, and, I think I must resolve, every single day, that, I will do my very best to make our lives a happy, and, a successful one!

Sylvan, I do love you more each day, even when I'm not with you in person! What God has given us is something very wonderful...something to be cherished for the rest of our lives! I pray our life, together, will be a long and happy one!

Darling, I almost forgot to tell you about Mike, tonight. He was so cute and so terribly funny! He was sitting on Grandma's lap, and, all of a sudden, he was all smiles, and, started laughing. He would look over at Dad, and then, over to me, and say "Shirley...Sylvan" and, then, he would laugh real hard, and say the same thing over again! He is about the cutest kid!

Darling...tomorrow morning I will be going to Church, and, during that short time, you and I will be closer to God then any other time of the day. I, do, cherish the times we went to church together!

Darling, I do love you with all of my heart and soul. There will never be another you...you are My Everything All my love...all my life

Shirley

P. S. I love you, deeply!

A MISERABLE AN HEARTBREAKING SITUATION

The next few letters in February were very miserable, heart breaking and sad for Sylvan & Shirley. They wanted to be married as soon after her graduation as was possible, however, her folks wanted her to wait at least a year, after her graduation before she went right into marriage. They thought she was too young for marriage yet. Of course, you can understand that she was their own little girl, and they were on the verge of losing her. Mom and Dad didn't want to let her go, yet. After all, she would be moving over 1400 miles away. It must have been, awfully hard, for them too! There was heartache on both sides! I have decided to omit a couple of those letters!

Sylvan decided to write her parents a letter, asking their consent! His next letter includes the answer to his letter...

February 23, 1953

Ft. Walton, Fla.

Just a short letter to let you know, that, I got Mom's letter, today. I can't say, that, it made me happy, and, I can't say it answered my question, either! I'm going to quote, word for word, what she said, so, you can know, exactly, what she said, and, there won't be any mix-ups! I'm not going to answer her letter until I receive your letter on Wednesday night!

Here is your Mother's letter:

"Dear Sylvan

Dad and I received your letter several days ago. I meant to answer sooner, but, I have been so busy. Mike had to be taken to the doctor, again, yesterday. They are going to take him to Omaha Monday to a doctor. The medicine didn't seem to help any, and, he hasn't been out of the house for over a week!

I presume Shirley wrote you, that, Everett was home over the week end, and, needless to say, we were, all, happy!

Sylvan, I thought I made it plain to you, when you were here, that, Dad and I feel Shirley is too young to marry. We want her to live a little before she takes on the responsibility of a home and family. We aren't trying to keep you apart. I want Shirley to know her own mind, without influence from you. You know she is going to graduate, and, that is a big time in any girls life! I think a wedding is sacred too, and should have it's place! I'm sure the time won't seem too long to you. We, all, have to make sacrifices, and, giving Shirley up, now, when our boys are all leaving, would be tough on Dad & I too. We will be happy to have you come in May, and hope, you feel, that, we want you to stay, here, at the house. We don't have the best, but, are glad to share it!

Roger writes that, he will be home in June, but, thinks he might be shipped out, anytime!

Shirley received your package this morning. The mail seems to be a little slow, at times. I must get busy, as, I'm trying to finish the mending.

I'm going to Omaha with Merle, Monday. Merle's car isn't up to the trip, so, I am taking mine!

Give my best regards to your Grandmother.

Sincerely,

Mom Baker

My Darling, I don't agree with your Mother, about some of those things! I don't think you do, either. For instance, about you being too young. If you _really_ love me, and, I know you do, there is no such thing as being _too young!_ Next...what kind of a living does she want you to have before you get married, if you're not happy? If you are miserable, all the time we are apart, what kind of a living do you call that?

You told me, you wanted the privilege of being my wife, and, having that responsibility. She says they are not trying to keep us apart. Well, what do you call it? They want you to know your own mind. They think you are still a little girl! You, definitely, know your own mind, don't you? They don't want me to influence you! That, My Dear, is what every man, from the beginning of time, has had to do to get that special girl to marry him. If we hadn't met and falling in love, you would, never have, agreed to marry me, if I hadn't asked you...would you? Yes, I guess you would, at that, for, we loved each other, mutually, and, it was, understood, from the beginning, that, we would be married, someday! She says a wedding has its place! Yes, any place, two people in love can get married! She says...She is sure the time won't seem long to me. How long? My Dear, it's been too long, already! God knows, we have suffered tortures, already, since we have been so far apart! She says several other things, but, I don't want to say, any thing else! You read the letter!

We have, already waited for 9 months, and it will, soon, be a year!

We can make our lives happy ones, and also, Mom and Dads, by telling them, we definitely plan to be married right after graduation. They will, eventually, be happy about it! They may, even, consent to it, if, they see, that, we are going to be married, regardless!

Oh, My Darling, it's not wrong for people, to fight for their happiness! Please see, that, it's our love and happiness, that, I am fighting for. I'll still love the folks after it is all over. They must not know, how much, you really love me! They haven't, really seen, how miserable, you really are! My Lovely Sweetheart, I do want you for my wife! That's all I'm fighting for. If I knew you didn't want me as badly, I wouldn't waste my time. Please remember, It's a poor man, who wouldn't fight for the one he loves, and, I love you, with everything I have! Please be mine, because...

I love only you!

Sylvan

P. S, <u>Love</u> Hath No Bounds!

Thursday night

February 26, 1953

Neligh, Nebr.

My Darling, I am writing, as promised, tonight.

Darling, I received your letter, this evening, telling me, you received Mom's letter. I want to answer, that first.

Darling, I do love you enough to stand behind you! It hurts, so, when you sound, that, maybe you are not sure. Please, Darling, you must know how I feel. I do want you. Darling you know I do!

Darling, thanks for giving me the exact words of Mom's letter. It certainly doesn't help things any,   (I mean, her letter.), and of course, I do agree with you. We don't agree on what she says, nor, I'm not too young! I've tried to prove, to her, how I feel, and, I don't know what I must do to make her understand! She sees, that, I am miserable and unhappy, for, she tells me to smile and laugh a little. She says I am mooning, and, you have influenced me, and, such things! I do have a mind of my own, and, a heart of my own! They, both, tell me, that, my happiness lies with you!

I hope I have made it clear...I am fighting for us, too, Dear! I know we have hurt each other in this fight for our happiness. After the heartache is over...I'm never going to hurt you one bit, not knowingly, at least!

By answering your letter of today, I have also answered the one I got yesterday, for, they are, basically, the same feelings.

Darling, the last few months in school are full ones! They would be filled with complete happiness, if, I knew, for sure, that we were going to marry after I graduate!

Darling, tomorrow night in the crowning of N. H. S. Sweetheart. Since I am an attendant, who knows, maybe, The "Sweetheart." It will be a very nice thing, but, perfect, only, if you were here to tell me you love me, and to be, in the crowd, watching the ceremonies. And, your eyes could be following me. I'd know they were on me, and, I would find you in the crowd. Darling, I most certainly, will be thinking of you, as always!

Write Mom, again, and tell her how we, both, feel! Just say what you think is best!

All my love, always. (believe this)

Shirley,
P. S. I love only you!
P. P. S. Thanks for the "Love Hath No Bounds"

March 4, 1953

Ft. Walton, Fla.

My Dearest Shirley,

The days are bringing us closer together, and, our love is growing more and more for each other, as the days pass.

It is, very hard waiting to hold you in my arms, and, tell you how much I love you! I'll, always, love you,

with everything I have!

Dear, I didn't get your letter, today, as I usually do. I suppose the mails were held up. I will, probably get it tomorrow morning. I did get your letter Monday, though. The extra letter, that, you wrote last Thursday evening. It made me a little happier than usual.

I'm so very happy, that, you do love me enough to stand behind me. I knew you did, but, I had to hear you say it, yourself, since we have been going through this turmoil. I'm very sorry I hurt you by saying..."if you want me." But I did have a reason for saying it, which, I will explain to you later, when we are together! I knew you want me, as much as, I want you. Please forgive me, My Dear, if I say things like that! They are not to hurt you, believe me

I will, probably, wait until this Sunday, to write Mom & Dad again. I will wait and see, what has developed there. I will let them know, just how we, both, feel, and, express our desire to marry soon after your graduation.

If they don't consent to us marrying right after your graduation, we will let them know, that, we plan to marry, with or without their consent, but that we, do, want their consent, and, we are hoping they will reconsider, and, make everyone happy. They must realize, that, we will be married, regardless! The reason we are asking is to make them happy too! There is no reason to wait!

Darling, I know you have tried to show Mom, how much you love me, but, she hasn't, really, stopped to think, how much it's hurting you! Why?

No, Darling, I too, believe, that, this is one sacrifice you don't need to make. It is their place to make this sacrifice, for we need to be together as soon as possible as much as we love each other!

Darling, just remember, that, they love you very much, and, it will hurt them, at first, but, they will get over it pretty soon.

Yes, Sweetheart, you have, definitely, made it clear, that, you are fighting for us. I'm so, very, proud of that fact! I, do, love you so very much, and, it helps a lot more, to know, that, you will fight for us! I'll be fighting, too!

Yes, darling, I do think Mom & Dad likes me fairly well, and I love them too, but, you are the one I want to marry, not them, therefore, I am fighting to get you! I do need you so, and, I am very lonesome for you. I'll always be lonesome, for you, when you are away from me!

Darling, I know you love me enough. I have not doubted your love for me. You have proven that fact!

Darling, I'll never hurt you again, either, after all this heartache is over. We are, really, not hurting each other, it's the obstacles in the way!

I, too, wish I could have been at the crowning of the N. H. S. sweetheart. It would have been wonderful to watch you, My Sweet Darling!

I will love you forever, and, I want to show you in person, not from afar, as we are now! When one is, really, in love, no one or nothing can stop them, because, as I said, before, "Love Hath No Bounds!"

All my love, always, and the day after!

Sylvan

P. S. I love you so very much!

P. P. S. Please marry me soon!

The crowning of the queen

February 28, 1953

Neligh, Nebr.

My Darling Sylvan,

I received your letter this morning. Thanks! You seemed to be a little less heartsick. I know you feel the same, but, the first real hurt is over! You haven't, yet, received my letter I wrote Thursday, but, you will find more of what you are looking for, in that, you know. I hope, that, you know I, do, love you so

much, and, nothing has, or, nothing can kill my love for you!

Darling, the very nicest thing that could happen to a girl in her Senior School life, happened to me last night. I was crowned N. H. S. Sweetheart or Queen! Oh, it made me so happy. If only, you could have been here to see the ceremony. It was so beautiful! Mother said, "Wouldn't Sylvan, have  been proud to see you sitting on that Throne!" Then, she said, that, you would say..."Nobody else could have been queen, when she is around!"

Darling, it did make me feel so good to know I am liked, well, by most of the students! There were 10 of us girls. We wore formals! We came through the gym door, one at a time...through a candle lit aisle, and, met  one of the basketball boys, took their arm, and, walked up a large candle lit aisle to the front of the gym. The aisles were lined by "N" club boys holding candles! In front of the gym, they announced, I was the

Sweetheart! No one, except 1 teacher and two boys had known, before it was announced! I was asked to step forward, and, Keith Petersen, the honorary Captain crowned me with a pretty crown, then, presented me with an "N" with N. H. S. Sweetheart "53" on it... That, I shall treasure for it is hard earned by the boys in sports. He presented me with a heart box of candy. The stage curtains were drawn open, and, the escorts took us to our thrones! It was the most beautifully decorated, than it has ever been! My throne was covered with blue velvet, and, there was a, beautiful, large heart, in back of me! I plan on sending you some pictures when I get them.

I have, at least, given you a fair picture of this!

It, really, made me happy! How perfect it would have been, if you had been there!

Darling, I love you so much.

I'm writing you this letter in the kitchen for I don't want to disturb the others.

Mike has been in the hospital, and, he and Myla are sleeping in my room. I am sleeping in the boy's room!

Darling, I have been so lonesome for you! Don't think I forgot you, during my happiness last night! How I was wishing you were in the crowd watching me!

Darling this whole letter has, practically been, all about the "Sweetheart" deal, but, you are my Sweetheart, and, I want you to know all the things that help my happiness! When we are together, you and I will, always, be a picture of happiness. Our love is so special! How can we help, but, be happy, if we, both, try to overcome every day trials, that will, naturally, arise. We have such a strong love!

Darling, how are your family? We have been so upset, lately, that we haven't mentioned them. Darling, I do hope they understand, there is a reason for the unhappiness, they have seen in your eyes, lately!

Darling, I too, have thought about the things we could be doing this summer. You can teach me how to swim. We could go dancing, to shows, to football games and Other things! I, most certainly, do not, think, that, married life is, just, going places. I, do, realize the responsibilities.

Darling, I love you very much. With all my heart and soul...never forget that! I want you as soon as possible!

All my love, for all my life!

Shirley

P. S. I'm crazy in love with you!

Ft. Walton, Fla.

My Darling Shirley

I received your sad, but, sweet letter today, and also, one Friday. The long one Friday was a wonderful letter. It, really shows, how you really feel, and what, an extra special person you are. You're so understanding and considerate of everyone. Darling, I'm so happy that you have a good heart. I love everything you are, and stand for! I know, I'll never have to doubt you, for, you are so honest and sincere in everything you do! Please, always stay that way! Your last two letters made me very sad, and, unhappy, for, you are, really, going through hell, even more so, than I am, because, you have to be right in the middle of this whole thing! I sure do hate, that it, all, had to be the way it is, but, shortly, it will be, all over, and it will be a happy future for us! Right?

My Sweet Darling, I know you don't want to hurt me, and, you're not hurting me. I know, if it were up to you, you would marry me as soon I get there!

My Dear, you do explain yourself, very well, and sweetly, too! I'm so proud of your sweet way! So kind hearted. You are, truly, the person I've been looking for, all my life, everything, and, more than I can, really hope for, in a woman!

My Darling, let's try to put these sad things behind us, and, look to our wonderful happy future, together!

It's only 76 days until we will be in each others arms, once again! We know how we both feel, and, we, both, know, that, we'll be together, for a lifetime soon!

Your letter, tomorrow, may bring happier news!

My Dear, I am truly happy, that, you did cry, and, get some of the hurt out of your system. It, really does, help a lot! Please don't hold back, when you feel like crying! Cry!

Business has been good, and, I'm getting some of our bills paid up!

I've sold quite a few lots out at Sylvania Heights! I'll tell you about it, later when I see you in May.

Carmen and Kip are, both, staying at our house for awhile, probably for several weeks.

Well, Sweetheart, the time has come, again, to say goodnight. I do hate to say goodnight to you, My Darling, for I miss you so very much, when you are away from me. I love you, truly, and, I'll, always love you, no matter what happens!

I'm yours forever,

Sylvan

P. S. I think of you constantly in everything I do!

March 6, 1953

Ft. Walton, Fla.

My Darling Shirley,

Just a short letter, to let you know, I received your Wednesday letter, yesterday. It was a very sweet one! I want to congratulate you, on the wonderful honor bestowed upon you, by your High School! Darling, I'm so proud of my wonderful Sweetheart and Queen!

I couldn't see how you wouldn't be crowned Queen. I just sort of had the feeling you would, because, you are so very sweet & wonderful!

My Darling, I do wish I could have been there to have seen you crowned Queen of N. H. S. I didn't see you, but, I was very proud of you sitting on the throne...My Queen!

> "If I had my way dear...forever there'd be
> A garden of roses for you and for me!
> A million and one things I would do,
> Just for you...Just for you...Just for you!
> If I had my way dear...forever there'd be
> Sunshine and laughter every day.
> And you'd reign all alone,
> Like a _Queen_ on a throne
> If I had my way!"

Sweetheart, how could you help being liked by so many people...when you have such a wonderful personality!

I am very proud, that, I have you for my very own!

Darling, I miss your kiss...the touch of your hand! I long to know, that, you understand...my buddy! I'll never want anyone but you, and, I want you soon!

All my love, always

Sylvan

P. S. I wish I were with you tonight...every night!

April 15, 1953

Neligh, Nebr.

My Darling,

Just think, just one month from tonight, we will be together. Oh, wonders of wonders! This time next month, I'll be in your arms!

Darling, I received your sweet letter this evening, when I came home. Every letter you write means so much to me!

Darling, your voice, too, was beautiful music to my ears. Those few minutes talk, with you, Sunday night, meant more to me than I can say. You will, always, be such a great comfort to me!

A very sad occasion

Darling, what makes wonderful, more wonderful, is the fact, that my parents, already, think the world of you! I believe they are happy, over the fact, that I have chosen (God has chosen) you for me, to marry!

Darling, it is so hard to write what I have to tell you

 about our darling Mike...He Just Died! Just 2 years old! We're going to miss that sweet little boy!

Darling, I know He meant so much to you. You belong to us, from the start. We are your family!

This afternoon, my girl friends and I went to Norfolk to shop. It felt good to relax a little.

I bought a cute little suit dress at half price. I am, really, satisfied. I will wear it to graduation, and naturally, especially for you. Maybe we will get to go to Norfolk again this time. I'll wear it, then. Too!

Oh, Darling, I received the vacation issue of the Playground Daily News...I enjoyed the Destin Page of familiar businesses and the boats and their owners...Thanks!

Darling, I will close, because it is late, and, the dining room light bothers the folks.

I love you, with, all of my heart and soul!

Now and forever, I'm yours,

Shirley

P. S. I love you immensely! Give my love to your family!

Sylvan's answer to Shirley's last letter

April 19, 1953

Ft. Walton, Fla.

My Sweet darling Shirley,

I love you every moment of each day. I don't know how I live without you with me at all times. I know, that, our love for each other will always be as great as it is now!

My Darling, my heart aches for Merle and Myla. Little Mike was such a sweet little boy! Yes, dear, he did mean a lot to me! We're, really, going to miss him!

Darling, thank you, very much, for saying that I belonged to your family from the start, and, that, I am family. It makes me so very happy! It is such a great joy, to know, that, I am loved by the family of the one I love so dearly! I shall never forget how wonderful they were to me, when I was there!

I, myself, hate to see you go to work, for the summer knowing, that, you should be here beside me! I'll have to admit it does hurt a little. However, I know that is not your wish, for, if you had your way, we would be together, forever, after graduation! I'm sorry, Darling, but, I'm just thinking and dreaming, on paper, it would be nice to have you soon! But, the best things are hardest to get and worth waiting for! _You are the best_, and worth waiting for!

It was nice, that, you got to go to Norfolk, with the

girls. I am longing to see you in your new suit dress.

I'll bet you look like a million dollars!

You bet we'll go to Norfolk, again, this time, and, more than once together, too. We'll go to other places, too. We won't have much time, so, we must make the best of it!

Well. My Sweet Darling Princess, I'll say goodnight, for now, and suffer tortures, until I get your Wednesday letter! I'm yours forever.

Sylvan

P. S. I love you, Shirley, with heart and soul!

Sylvan just finished his last letter in April, and, Shirley's next letter will be her last letter in April! Two more letters in May, will be all the letters to be used before Sylvan leaves for Nebraska on May 13.

April 20, 1953

Neligh, Nebr.

Dearest Sylvan,

I received your letter today, and, it made me extremely happy!

I have my own room back, again, tonight, and, from now on, I guess. I sure hope so. I can write to you and look at your picture, again, for a change! Merle and Myla found a place to stay and moved out!

I love you. Does that sound good to you? Silly question, huh?

Darling, several times, today, it has been mentioned, that there are only 4 weeks of school left. I figure, only 4 weeks of school means Sylvan, my Sylvan, will be here! Darling, on Saturday, May 15th I will be patiently waiting for you! Certainly, you should come right to our place, and, be staying with us. The whole family is planning on it!

Darling, I'm glad you received my letter, and, that you are happy. I hope, because of me! I know you are my happiness!

Sylvan, I feel as you feel, I wonder, sometimes, if I can wait until these last few weeks pass and you are here, holding me, kissing me...just being near me! How wonderful it shall be! I love you!

214

Darling, I have, really, been feeling good today. My skin isn't so bad.

Darling, your letter, today, was so wonderful. I feel like thanking you for each and every letter. They mean so much, when we can't see each other personally!

I wish you were here, as always. I know you will be here, before too long!

Dearest, please take care of your self. We have a long, happy life together, yet! I love you.

Shirley

P. S. Thanks for being mine!

The next 2 letters will be the last letters in this book! Sylvan will be leaving for Nebraska on Thursday may 13th. The next letter will be Sylvan's last letter. The following letter will be Shirley's last letter in the book!

May 6, 1953

Ft. Walton, Fla.

My Darling Sweet Shirley,

What a wonderful occasion. It will be, just, 8 nights from tonight, and, I'll be in the arms of my darling. It is hard to wait!

I, just, got your sweet letter, today, on time, and, it made me want to leave tomorrow morning instead of next Thursday morning. I love you very much, and, I do

215

want to be with you.   How can we wait another 3 months?

Darling I got Mom's letter.   Please thank her for inviting me to stay at your home while I am in Neligh.

Tell her, I am, also, looking forward to my visit, and seeing all of you, again!

Yes, My Sweet, one week from Saturday Night I will be there hugging and kissing you, if, I have anything to say about it!

Darling, I do know how you long to have me beside you, and, I can't see why we must wait another 3 months...I really can't! It will be nice to go out, lots together, just you and I alone. It will be wonderful to be free to do things we want to do together!

Dear, we can earnestly plan our future this trip.   It will be wonderful to be able to plan our wedding, while I am there!

It makes me feel so good, to know, that your future plans are for you and I.   I, do, want it that way forever...Please!

Yes, My Sweet, I will be careful, just for you, always, because, my pledge is, to always keep you happy in every way. If something were to happen to me, you would not be happy, right? Yes, Darling, we must have a happy life together, and, we haven't even started yet. As you said, we both must be careful, and, fight to keep our lives happy! If we do not get married this trip, the next three months will be so, very, unhappy and lonesome ones. It has been so hard this past year, being away from you. I can't stand it much longer, believe me, I must have you with me!

My Darling, you have been down in your last few letters, just as I have, but, I think they are wonderful, for, I, always, want you to pour your heart out to me, and cry on my shoulder! I, always, want to be the one to comfort you! Please know that I'll always be there for you!

Yes, Darling, I will stay at your house, while I am there. I do hope I'm not in the way, and, imposing on your folks. That's the last thing I want to do. I do love them.

Sweetheart, I have your rings in my possession, and, they are, really, beautiful. I'm crazy about them. I can hardly wait to give them to you, and, make you mine with them!

I'll be in your arms next week...soon...soon...soon I'll be in your arms. I love you so much,

Sylvan

P. S. Be all mine, soon. Please!

Shirley's short, but, sweet last letter for this book follows:

May 8, 1953

Neligh, Nebr.

My Darling,

Oh, I can hardly wait another week until you get here. How wonderful, it will be, to see you, to be with you, doing so many things together!

Just one more letter to write, then my Darling will be here!

Darling, my sunburn, I got the other day, is, really, a terrible mess. It burns, constantly. It has peeled down to flesh. What a mess. I only hope it doesn't make my eczema worse. I certainly hope it looks a little better by the time you get here!

Darling, I suppose you and Little Mother received my graduation announcements.

Darling, I am very lonesome for you! You know, exactly how I feel, I'm sure! Just one more week, but one can seem like ten, sometimes!

I am short on news, but, I always want to let you know, I love you with all of my heart and soul!

With all my love, I'm yours.

Shirley

P. S. I love you only!

The last letter concludes all of Sylvan and Shirley's letters of courtship by mail that will be used in this book!

The rest of the book will start with Sylvan preparing for:

Leaving Florida for Nebraska:

On Wednesday May 12, 1953 Sylvan got all of his business in order, brought all of his bills up to date, leased his sign business to his Sign Man, Jim, had his car serviced, went home and packed his bags!

Early Thursday morning May 13, 1953, about 4:30 a.m. Sylvan left Ft. Walton. He drove west to Mobile, Ala. Had breakfast, then Northwest through Jackson, Miss. Had lunch in Winona, Miss. Then North to Memphis, Tenn. Took 63 North Through the Ozarks to Jonesboro, Ark. Where he had supper and Spent the first night.

He left Jonesboro around 5:30 Friday morning on 63 and had breakfast in West Plains, Mo. He drove through Springfield, Mo. On up through to Kansas City, reading the numerous, different, Burma Shave signs as he drove. Sylvan had lunch just above Kansas City. After lunch he drove to Nebraska City about 50 miles south of Omaha, had supper and spent the second night.

About 6:30 am Saturday morning, he had breakfast and drove to Norfolk, Nebr. Had lunch, called Shirley, and told her, that, he would be there in less than an hour. He drove on to Neligh.

When he got out of the car, in front of the house, guess who came running out of the house to meet him...You guessed it! They embraced and kissed! Why not? He got a cordial welcome from the folks. It was the beginning of a new life to come! They, all, visited and watched T. V. for a while, prepared and had supper. After supper Sylvan resumed his job as dish washer!

After all the chores were finished, Sylvan and Shirley went for a drive around town to talk and to plan their future. Sylvan gave Shirley her engagement ring. Sylvan insisted on talking to her Mother in the next couple days, about their marriage, while he was here. Shirley agreed!

On Sunday afternoon, after lunch, Sylvan, Shirley and Mom Baker were sitting on the front porch talking!

Sylvan, finally, got up the nerve to ask..."Mom, Shirley and I have been talking about getting married for several months now. We love each other with all of our hearts, and, don't feel like we should have to wait much longer. We would like to be married right after her graduation, with your and Dad's consent, of course!" "Well, I don't know if we can let her go, yet. She is kind of young!" Mom Replied.

"Mom, Shirley is 181/2 years old and has a mind of her own! I know it is going to be hard for you and Dad, to see, your only little girl moving a long way away from home, but, I'll bring her back home as often as I can!" "Well, I'll have to ask Dad and see what he has to say about it." Mom Said. Mom went and talked to Dad. A while later, Mom came back with the answer..."Dad said, that, we might as well let them get married, because, they'll probably get married anyway!" Right after that, the preparations began to take shape!

Sylvan paid the price

In the mean time, Sylvan felt like he ought to do something to "pay" for Shirley! Ha! Ha! The outside of their house had needed painting for a long time. Sylvan told Dad, if he got the Paint he would paint the outside of the house! As you can see, by the picture, it was a big house. In the next few days, Sylvan had it painted! The whole exterior!

He wouldn't have to worry about taking her now, He paid the price! Ha! Ha!

They set the date of the wedding for Saturday June 5. at 2:00 pm. Sylvan and Shirley started their list for the announcements, for both sides of the families, and friends, and sent them out.

They decided not to plan a Big Church Wedding, but, to have the wedding in the Family Room of the Baker home. Sylvan & Shirley didn't, especially, want a big, expensive, Church Wedding, anyway.

Mom asked the Pastor of the Methodist Church to perform the wedding. He agreed!

Shirley chose Jacque as her Maid of Honor and Sylvan chose Merle as his best man!

We'll leave the preparations of the wedding ceremony for a little while, and start preparing for the, next, most important thing of Shirley's life, and that's her graduation ceremony on the May 25. It was a beautiful graduation ceremony. Shirley wore that cute suit dress that she had bought in Norfolk last month, on April 15th, when she went shopping with her girl friends. Boy, she did look beautiful, as usual!

The next few days, before, the graduation ceremony and the few days after graduation and before the wedding, Sylvan and Shirley spent a lot of time together. Besides doing the chores, around the house, during the daytime, they went downtown to look around and to do some shopping. They spent

some time in the corner Walgreen's soda fountain. A couple of times they drove all the way to Norfolk to get themselves a hot fudge sundae at Dairy Queen!

Not too long after graduation, Shirley's girl friends had a bridal shower for her. (See picture above) I think the shower was held at Kathryn Hildreth's home, but, I'm not sure. Sylvan drove her there and picked her up, afterwards. She got a lot of beautiful gifts!

The Wedding

------Exchanging of Rings!
Pronounced Man & Wife
Embraced & Kissed!-------

-----Sylvan & Shirley posing,
after the wedding!

Sylvan & Shirley with
  Mom & Dad Baker!----------

----Mom &
Dad Baker

Sylvan & Shirley
  With the Pastor------

Sylvan & Shirley with
Jacque & Merle--------

---------Shirley & Sylvan with
her 3 Closest girl friends
Kathy, Kathryn, & Kay Lou.

The Reception

The Beautiful
------Wedding Cake

Sylvan & Shirley
Cutting the cake----

---Shirley feeding
Sylvan

Sylvan feeding
Shirley-----

They received many nice gifts, including, a bit of cash money, from the folks and relatives!

Sylvan & Shirley in Downtown Neligh with their wedding garments on!

Why they are in Downtown Neligh with their wedding garments on is a mystery to me! I don't remember! Maybe they had some pictures made! They are in front of the studio!

The Get-Away (The Honeymoon)

Shirley & Sylvan getting ready to leave town. Merle is cleaning off the door handle, so they can get in the car! The car was lettered with black & white shoe polish! Fresh & sticky!

Oh happy day...finally on their way!

Sylvan and Shirley left Neligh around 5:30 pm June 5th, and drove 35 miles east to Norfolk. They spent their first night at the Madison Hotel in Norfolk. Sunday Morning June 6, they drove to Sioux City, Iowa, where they spent several days. They found a gas station, on the Missouri River, that had a car wash. Normally, a car wash in those days was $1.00 to a $1.50. They charged $8.00. That, really, hurt, because they didn't have much money left. Of course, shoe polish is very hard to get off! Anyway, Sylvan & Shirley shopped and saw a couple of movies while they were in Sioux City! One of those movies was "Peter Pan", a very good movie!

About June 10th they started back to Neligh. On the way back they ran into some severe weather, with a lot of wind, rain and churning black clouds, overhead! Thank God, they were able to get back to Neligh, Safely. In the paper, the next morning, there, were reports of Tornados that had touched down in different places. They, also, had a picture, in the paper of that gas station on the Missouri River in Sioux City that had been overflowed with Water! I wonder!

Sylvan & Shirley spent a couple more days with Mom & Dad before they prepared to leave for Florida. It was going to be a very hard experience for Mom and Dad for a long while after Sylvan and Shirley left, as well as for Shirley, too! Sylvan assured them, that, he would take good care of Shirley. "Mom, Dad, we love you, two, very much. We love each other with all of our hearts, and have, from the very beginning! I know, that, you are very proud of Shirley! She is the sweetest girl I know! You can be assured, that, I will take, good, care of her, and, treat her like a Queen, because she is my Queen! I will bring her back to Neligh as often as possible!"

Homeward bound

Sylvan and Shirley left Neligh early on Monday Morn. June 14th. They drove on U. S. 275 to Omaha, on 73 to Kansas City. From Kansas City they drove through Springfield, Mo. On U. S. 65 To about 100 miles south of Springfield, where they spent the first night around Harrison, Ark. About 500 miles from Neligh.

(I'd like to tell you readers the fact, that, the Interstate Highway System was just being started, across the Country, so, there were no Interstates to travel on, in most of the country, in the '50's!)

Tuesday morning they drove about 2 hours and had breakfast. As they drove, on U. S. 65 toward Little Rock After breakfast, they noticed some, very dark clouds ahead! The radio was turned on, and, reports of possible tornados were in the forecast! As they neared Little Rock, real dark churning clouds appeared over the mountains from the Southwest. There was a store & gas station, just ahead on the left. They pulled in, and, parked in front of the store!

A man came running out of the store, toward their car and shouted, "Hurry up, get out of your car and come inside, we're going down into our cellar...there is a tornado headed toward us!" They did as he said, and, went down into the cellar with them. Sylvan & Shirley were, two scared young people, wondering about their car, and, all of their belongings, would they still be out there, after the storm?

They sat, with their arms around each other until the storm was over. The man opened the cellar door and looked out! It was over! The storm had crossed, between them and Little Rock. Their car was still sitting there, thank God! They thanked the people, got into their car (It was about 9 am) and drove through Little Rock on 65 to U. S. 82, crossed over the Mississippi River to Greenville, Miss., and had lunch.

After lunch they drove down 61 to 80, on 80 East to Jackson, Miss., then on 49 to Hattiesburg, Miss. They spent the second night in Hattiesburg. The next day, they drove the rest of the way to Ft. Walton. They arrived home on June 17th, in the late afternoon! Boy, were they happy to be home! They were dog tired! Shirley was, about as tired as she had been in a long time! As soon as they got home, they called the Folks and told them they were home!

For the rest of their lives!

For the next 20 or so pages, I'm going to try to give you readers some highlights of Sylvan & Shirley's long and wonderful love life together.

Don't get me wrong, because, their physical and financial life was not a bed of roses! However, their love for each other grew as the years rolled by, and, their love for each other, was just as great, at the end, as it was in the beginning.

When I talk about their physical life, I am referring to Shirley's lifetime bout with her eczema. It plagued her more as the years went by. It hadn't been mentioned, before, in this book, but, Sylvan was a bronchial asthmatic, all of his life. Both diseases are caused by different kinds of allergies. Sylvan's allergies were not as critical as was Shirley's. Shirley's allergies were <u>almost</u> uncontrollable, whereas, Sylvan's is controlled by Ipratropium Bromide and Albuterol Sulfate Inhalers!

When I talk about their financial lives, it had its ups and downs. As you know, at the beginning of this book I mentioned that Sylvan was in the sign business. He was in the sign business for 60 years, From December 1947, until he had his by-pass heart surgery in December 2007! The business was closed after that, never to open again! There were good years and bad years. More and more competition as the years went by! Less & less business!

Their love for each other over shadowed any adversities that came up in life. They were happy with each other!

Well, let's settle Sylvan and Shirley down in their little, self made, one bedroom, one bathroom block house, surrounded by scores of all kinds of trees at 330 Elliott Road in East Ft. Walton. Those trees put out lots of pollen, at certain times of the year!

After they were in the house a few days they had to find a place for Little Mother, Sylvan's Grandmother, to stay. They finally acquired a small 1 bedroom trailer that they set up on the Northeast section of their lot, under many trees! She lived there for several months, she then, moved to a low rent apartment complex in Pensacola.

The next day after Sylvan & Shirley arrived home they went down to the Sign Shop to see how Jim was doing, and found the shop closed up! Jim had moved out and went into business for himself in another location in town! That's great! Now Sylvan had to start all over to get his customers back. It didn't take long, for, he had some loyal customers, and, it had only been a couple of weeks! Eventually Jim moved out of town!

Planning their future

Sylvan & Shirley, slowly, settled down into their little home and new environment! It took a while for Shirley to adjust to being away from her family, and, she got lonely & homesick, from time to time.

Happy Sylvan & Shirley in front of their window air conditioner, in the living room of their little block home. Note their wedding picture on the right hand corner of the air conditioner! When they get through posing for this picture, they will begin to plan their future in Ft. Walton: They planned their future family...A new addition to their house and other things. Shirley said she wanted, at least, five or six children, but, they were able to have, only, two girls: Jo Elaine, born on November 18, 1954 & Mary, born on June 12, 1957. A couple years after Mary was born in 1957, the doctor told Shirley, that, her womb was not in good enough condition to conceive another child. A couple years later her womb collapsed and dropped. She had to have a hysterectomy operation to remove the necessary organs!

The new addition to their house was to begin in late 1953 and included a large master bedroom, a large living room and a one car garage. The house had very high gables. They called the house, "The Marler Gables!" They estimated, that, it would take about 3 to 4 months to complete! The new addition was covered, outside, with red brick!

In their planning, they planned a trip back to Nebraska as soon as they could arrange it.

Probably, in the early summer 1954, after the new addition was finished. They did finish the new addition in the late spring of 1954. The bedroom and living room were decorated & furnished by Shirley's excellent taste!

In late March, 1954, Shirley found out, that, she was pregnant with their first child!

There were, now, two reasons to rejoice over their planning! The new addition to their house completed, and now a new addition to their family coming in a few months!

The third reason to rejoice is the fact, that, they were going to Nebraska in June to see all of the folks. This was to be the first of many trips to Nebraska. They made a trip, at least once, every year. Trips in the Summer, at Thanksgiving time and at Christmas time, in different years, of course!

When their first baby, Jo Elaine, was one year old

 they took a train to Nebraska, by way of Chicago. That was a trip they would never take again. At Chicago they had to wait several hours for the next train, and, they were very, very tired, worn out and weary, especially Shirley and the Baby!

 On one of their trips to Nebraska in 1960 when Jo Elaine was 6 and Mary was around 4, Dad & Mom Baker, Sylvan & Shirley and the 2 girls decided to take a trip up in to the Black Hills of South Dakota, to Mount Rushmore, by way of Wyoming. They spent one night with Shirley's Aunt and Uncle in Cheyenne. The picture at left was taken in front the Baker Home, before the trip to Mount Rushmore! It was about 11:00 a.m. when we got to the bottom of the Mountain. Dad Baker & Shirley, suggested, that they stop and get something to eat. (If they don't eat pretty close to meal time, it bothers them, because of their affliction.) Sylvan said, "Let's wait until we get up there, it'll only be about an hour." Ha! Ha! It took 3 hours! They didn't get there until 2 pm. It took Sylvan awhile to live that one down!

While they were on the winding highway up the mountain, they were stopped by several Bears on the highway, wanting a handout, but they wouldn't dare stop and open the windows. That made it, kind of slow traveling and a little scary, too!

They were still carving the faces of the Presidents on the side of Mount Rushmore at that time!

Many Anniversary/Vacation Trips

Sylvan, Shirley and the girls took many trips to different places in the Southeast besides their trips to Nebraska, over the years, until the girls were married in the early 70's. Usually, most of their trips were taken in the first part of June to coincide with their Wedding Anniversary! Their favorite food, on their wedding anniversary, was prime rib, salad and baked potato!

They went up to Gatlinburg, Tenn., several times by way of Cherokee, N. C.   They stopped at the Cherokee Indian village, so, that the girls could see the Indians, and, have their pictures taken with them, then, over the Smoky Mountains. They got out of the car and stood by some of the many mountain streams before they got to Gatlinburg...What a pleasure!

In October of 1996, 3 older couples... John & Betty Martin, Jack & Lorene Cartwright, and Sylvan & Shirley went up to Gatlinburg, while all of the leaves on the trees were changing color...What a beautiful sight!

In 1968, Sylvan, Shirley, the girls & young Cindy Marshall, a friend of the girls, visited Busch Gardens in Tampa Florida. They rode on the monorail around the gardens, and saw the Giraffes and other animals!

In 1972 the family visited Disney World, just after it opened! It was a very enjoyable vacation.

Several years Later, Sylvan and Shirley visited Sea World, and, then over to Disney World & Epcot Center, the City of many Nations! They had fun!

Besides going up to Neligh to visit Mom & Dad and family, Mom & Dad came down to Ft. Walton Beach, to visit Sylvan & Shirley, early each year, for several years. The first few years, they traveled by train. The last couple of years they traveled by plane. While they were in Florida, Sylvan & Shirley, occasionally, took them, on a trip, to other places. One year they went up to Chattanooga, Tenn. to Lookout Mountain. One year to Silver Springs. One year over to Homosassa Springs! One year down to Weeki Wachee Springs. One year to Orlando and down to Miami. One year to Bellingrath Gardens near Mobile! Etc. etc.

I've got several other vacation spots to take you to, a little later, but, I need to take you back into Shirley's physical life, that has caused her so much distress over the years, without, friends and loved ones hardly knowing about it! You see, Shirley never complained about <u>her</u> affliction. She was more concerned about helping other friends and loved ones in their problems, because, she was such a sweet and loving person! As years went by, she <u>couldn't</u> help others at all!

As I mentioned, several times, in this book, her eczema bothered her more and more, as the years went by! She attended several dermatologists to try to find some cure or relief! They prescribed different medicines. They would help for a little while, then, her eczema would start again! About 6 years after Sylvan and Shirley were married they had a prescription filled at the drug store and the druggist filled it with the wrong medicine. Shirley got real sick and went into hallucinations. They had to take her to the emergency room, with the prescription. Her Doctor informed her, that, it was <u>not</u> the medicine he prescribed. He treated her with something to help her get straightened out. She stayed sick for several weeks. Her head was, still, not too clear, because of that wrong medicine.

Sylvan couldn't take care of the children because of his work. They called Mom Baker and asked her to come down and help out. She did. Mom Baker couldn't stay very long, so, she decided to take Shirley and the girls back to Neligh and have her treated up there. After Sylvan got his work caught up, he, too, went up to Neligh. They put Shirley in a hospital in Norfolk. Her head was still not too clear. The doctors thought she was losing her mind, so, they wanted to put her in a mental institution. Shirley, finally, convinced them, that, her mind was O. K. They put her under more tests, and, found out, she was right! In a few days, she was sent home to Neligh, and, after a few days Sylvan brought her and the girls back to Ft. Walton. Boy, what a trial and ordeal that was!

Shirley continued to have bouts with her affliction. She was in and out of the hospital from time to time.

Sylvan remembers, one time, when Shirley was in the old Ft. Walton Hospital on Hospital Drive. He took the Girls to see her, and, as they were driving home, and, as he turned left onto Hollywood Blvd., the right side pick-up truck door flew open and Jo Elaine, 10 years old, fell out. Sylvan, stopped the truck, jumped out, and started around the truck to check on her, but, he heard the truck door slam. Jo Elaine, had, already, jumped back into the truck, unhurt, and, closed the door. She did have a few small scratches. That was one of the scary, but, humorous things in their lives! Sylvan has never forgotten that!

Before I take you on some more enjoyable Vacations & Trips that Sylvan & Shirley were blessed with, I would like to tell you about another medical encounter that Shirley went through, that, was, a vary happy situation for a while, that eventually turned out to be a very sad time of her life!

In early 1969, after seeing several doctors, over the years, one doctor recommended a very highly educated Dermatologist in Pensacola that, was, experienced in all kinds of skin diseases. This particular doctor, (I won't give his name...), He was familiar with a drug called Corticosteroid! Other drug names connected with that drug, that was prescribed for Shirley, by that Doctor, were Cortisone and Dexamethasone. The Cortisone did wonders for her skin for several years. That was the happy situation.

Now, I'm going to tell you about the sad part about that situation...In 1978, Sylvan & Shirley took a wonderful vacation trip, up to Hendersonville, N. C., and the Area. They stayed in a cabin on Hwy. 9 at the foot of Chimney Rock, near Lake Lure. They visited a Pastor friends Church in Hendersonville on Wednesday night and Sunday!

One day they took a, site seeing excursion, on a pontoon boat around Lake Lure, very Nice! One day they were sitting in the cabin, resting. Sylvan was looking out of the back window, at the side of the mountain. Suddenly he exclaimed..."I think I see little specks moving on the side of that mountain. I'm going next door, to the manager's office, and see if he has a pair of binoculars." He came back with the binoculars and looked up at the side of the mountain, and sure enough there were people walking on a trail on the side of that mountain.

Sylvan said to Shirley, "You like to walk, would you like to go up there, tomorrow, and walk down that trail?" "That, really, would be nice!" Shirley Replied. Now, here is the sad & unhappy part of this story. After they got back to the Cabin, from their walk on the mountain side, and cleaned up...Shirley started combing and brushing her beautiful long brunette hair, and her hair started coming out in her comb and brush. Oh my, what an awful feeling that was for her and for Sylvan...A possibility that she was going to lose her hair. They, both, cried! The next day they started back home. Every time she combed her hair, a little more would come out! She

finally lost all of it. She found out, from the Doctor, that, it is possibly, a side effect from the Cortisone. She tried using all kinds of wigs, but, the wigs made her head itch, too much. She, finally, came up with her own designs of some beautiful & colorful head pieces that matched the clothes that she wore, like the one at left, for the rest of her life! They were very pretty on that Pretty Lady!

Well, let's move from that sad episode to some more pleasant & enjoyable times along the journey to the end of this wonderful love story, with some happiness & sadness, along the way!

After they take a few more trips of very enjoyable vacation times, combined, with their wedding anniversaries, I'll tell you about the sad, but, happy ending of this love story book!

237

They took several anniversary/vacation trips up to Helen, Georgia, Alpine Swiss German Village Where they stayed at the Riverside Motel, right beside the Chattahoochee River. The picture on the left was

taken in the early 90's, and the one on the right was taken in the mid 90's. You can see the river in the background of the pictures.

At Helen, they ate their (anniversary) prime rib at a large Restaurant on Hwy. 75 by the Chattahoochee

River. On one trip to Helen, they went up to see the Anna Ruby Falls. Another trip, they went up to a Sheep Ranch, North of Helen. It was unique, in the fact, that, its activities were based on the Bible. Even the Sheep would come when the man would yell the word, "Hallelujah", the Sheep would come running toward him! "My sheep know my voice!" Another enjoyable sight was the beautiful flower gardens in Hiawassee, Ga., A few miles north of Helen. Their Daughter Mary and her husband Anthony were with them, on those two events. The sheep ranch and Hiawassee!

They went up to Branson, Mo., on a couple of occasions. The first time in 1995 they saw

several of the shows and then over to Eureka Springs and saw the live Passion Play. It was beautiful! In 1998 they saw several of the shows, and, also, they took a cruise on the Showboat Branson Belle. Shirley said that was for Sylvan's 75ᵗʰ Birthday!

In June, 2001 they went up to Lake Martin near Dadeville, Ala., Where they spent several days. It was, really beautiful on the lake as you can see by  the pictures. (The pictures <u>were</u> in beautiful color.) The picture at left is the front of the unit, that, Sylvan & Shirley stayed in. The picture of the Lake, on the right, was taken from in front of their unit.

 Sylvan took the picture of Fran Nolte, the Manager of the resort and Shirley sitting in front of their unit. Mrs. Nolte, really, liked Shirley, as <u>all</u> people do! Sylvan sure does. No! He loves her!

Sylvan & Shirley ate at a couple of Eateries in Dadeville. They had pretty good food!

Sylvan & Shirley loved to stop at the Cracker Barrel, to eat, on all of their trips, wherever they were available, when they were ready to eat...Breakfast, Lunch or Supper. They always enjoyed the good food there!

The Golden Anniversary

In the year 2003 was their 50ᵗʰ Wedding Anniversary! (Golden). That was real special! It's going to take a while, to tell you about it, with several pictures!

What a wonderful 50ᵗʰ Anniversary Wedding Party that was! It was planned by their families, their oldest Daughter, Jo, and, her Husband Ken, and, their youngest Daughter Mary, and, her Husband Anthony. It was held at Jo & Ken's home at 54 Cape Drive in Ft. Walton Beach, Fla. Many of their loved ones, and Friends were in attendance.

Granddaughter Elizabeth pinned on the flowers

--Shirley/Sylvan--

-----The beautiful cake-goodies & more goodies!

Shirley & Sylvan Looking at the Cake-------

Waiting to cut the Cake-------

Cutting the Cake-----------

Shirley feeding Sylvan

Sylvan feeding Shirley

Drinking the Punch-----

Opening the Gifts

Besides giving Sylvan & Shirley this wonderful 50th Anniversary Party, the families leased them a time share condominium in Cleveland, Ga. About 10 miles south of Helen At the:

Mountain Lakes Resort Country Hideaway Condominium overlooking the big lakes!

Their unit was a 2 bedroom apartment, with bathroom, bedroom, kitchen, stove, micro wave, refrigerator, televisions, etc.

--------Sylvan by the Lake

Shirley by the Lake--------

There are many more pictures of the lakes and buildings, but, that will be all I'll show, in this book, for the 50th Golden vacation.

While Sylvan & Shirley were on that 50th anniversary Vacation, The family painted the living room & halls of their home!

The next Anniversary vacation was in June, 2004, in Apalachicola, Fla., At the House of Tartts. They stayed there 5 nights. There were a couple of good Seafood Restaurants, right on the Bay, which ran right into the Gulf of Mexico! Fresh hot Seafood! Wow!

Their June 2005 vacation was, also, in Apalachicola. They stayed at the Bryant House Bed & Breakfast! It was a little different at the Bryant House, the bed was king size and was more than 3' high. Shirley had to have a small step stool to get in bed. They did, almost, the same things on that vacation, as they did the year before!

In June 2006, they spent a few days in Fairhope, Ala. They spent 5 nights at Barons Inn, on Mobile Street, & near the City Park, both by the Mobile Bay. They sat, &, walked in the Park. They ate all their meals in a Fairhope Restaurant that had good home cooked meals.

Shirley went shopping for some special clothes she wanted. They noticed a little ladies shop two doors down from the restaurant, called "The Cats Meow." They tried it, but they didn't have what she wanted. The Lady at the store suggested, that, she try the "Town & Country Store." She gave Shirley the address, and, they went over there. The Town &

Country had lots of clothes Shirley liked. Shirley picked out a couple of things! While they were there, they ask the Lady if she knew of a nice place to stay, next year, if they come back. She had a partner, that, was an older Lady, in her Eighties, that had, a Cabin, on her lot, with her home, right on Mobile Bay. Her name is Bessie Montgomery, Widowed! They got her address and phone number, and went down to see the Cabin. It was nice, with 2 bedrooms, with T. V.'s in each bedroom! Living room with T. V., Kitchen, Bathroom & Dinette and a car port!

In June 2007, was also, spent in Fairhope, Ala. This time they <u>did</u> stay at Bessie Montgomery's Cabin! By this time, Shirley was on a walker, hurting. She had fallen off a secretarial type chair in February 2007 and hurt her back. They talked about not going on the trip, but, Shirley insisted, saying, "It will be good for us to get away, for a spell!" They did basically, the same things, as they did before. That was their last Anniversary Vacation, together, as you will find out, why, later as I finish the book!

I'm going to take you back a few years to 1968...I mentioned earlier in the book, that their property at 330 Elliott Road had lots of trees, with lots of pollen. In early 1968 they were convinced that they were both very allergic to the pollens from the trees and, very reluctantly, decided, that, they needed to move away from that location, so they listed their property with a realtor. In the meantime Sylvan's Dad, "Poppa Bill", was selling his property in Destin...The Marlborough Motel & Cottages. "Poppa Bill and "Mamma Sibyl", both, liked Sylvan & Shirley's property, and offered to buy it. Sylvan & Shirley found a small 4 bedroom home, on the other side of town, at 37 Temple Ave. They bought it, and moved there in August, 1968, with their 2 daughters, of course. They have lived there for 41 years! Sylvan still lives there.

On the next couple of pages I'm going to enter a collage of 10 or 12 interesting pictures...

FROM REAL YOUNG TO GROWING
OLDER GRACEFULLY

Mom & Shirley

Shirley & Sylvan
Before Marriage

Shirley & Sylvan &
6 Months Jo Elaine

12 Months Jo Elaine

4 year Jo Elaine

1 Year Mary

5 year Jo Elaine

2 ½ year Mary

Sylvan & Shirley
with Bob & Sandra Brown
At Anthony & Mary's Home
Retired Pastor after 40 years

On one trip, while Sylvan & Shirley were visiting in Neligh, they took this picture of Shirley's handsome family, in the family room, around Moms Piano. They are from left to right...Roger, Merle, Shirley, Mom,

Dad, Larry behind Mom and Everett behind Dad! Only ones still living is Roger, Larry & families.

The Beginning of the End

As you know by now, from the beginning of this book, Shirley has been fighting her affliction with Eczema!

As early as the early 90's, Shirley's body began to show the effects of the medicine, Cortisone. It began to take a toll on her whole body. Besides losing her hair in 1978, her body joints were beginning to show signs of aches and pains. The Cortisone was affecting the cushions in her joints. They were slowly deteriorating until bone was rubbing against bone.

Her toes and her fingers were slowly showing signs of twisting little by little! Bunions and calluses began to show on her outside toe joints. She had a hard time finding shoes that would fit! The skin, all over her body, got so thin that it wouldn't hold stitches when she had a cut or a tear. They had to be held together with fly stitches, until they healed, and that was slow.

As early as 2001, the heel of her shoes was rubbing the heel of her foot, until the ankle part of the Achilles tendon was showing and took months to heal. It was the same when her ankles got raw from the top back of her shoe heel rubbing them. They wouldn't heal. She found out, that, she had very little circulation in her lower legs and feet.

The Doctors could find very little pulse in her feet! In 2005, they sent Shirley to a new Doctor in town, who was a Board Certified Vascular Surgeon. After he had performed his examination, he told her that she had very little circulation in her left leg and foot, and that the main artery in her left leg was clogged. He said she did have some circulation and pulse in her right leg. He told her that the artery in her left leg would have to be replaced. He would have to do by-pass surgery on her left leg. He said it would help some, but, she would still have problems healing. He performed the surgery just before the hurricane

Ivan was predicted to hit the area. They had to send her home, during the storm, and back in the hospital, after the storm, for a couple more weeks.

After that, she was home for a while, under Gentiva home nursing care. In 2007, after they returned from their Fairhope Vacation, Shirley's back was hurting more & more. She had it x-rayed. They found a disc out of place, and a pinched nerve in her back! They couldn't operate because of her health.

Then in Mid September 2007 she fell out of bed and tore the skin on her leg, real bad. They rushed her to the ER. The Doctor patched her up and sent her home. That night, she got real sick and went into hallucinations! The next morning she was in a coma, and she had a high fever. Back to the Hospital where she stayed several days not expected to live, but she lived. She was, then, sent to The Parthenon Nursing Facility in Ft. Walton Beach for 6 months. On December 24, 2007, Sylvan had Heart by-pass surgery! After a several days in the hospital, he was sent to the same Health Care Center, and was in the same room with Shirley. After about 2 weeks, there, he contacted a serious, contagious, stomach disease called C-dif, and was sent back to the hospital, not expected to live, but he did. He wasn't ready to go yet. After a few days in the hospital, he and Shirley were, both, sent to the Destin Health Care and Rehab Center in Destin, Fl. on March 5, 2008 After 2 months there, they were, both, sent back home on May 12, 2008. Shirley spent 8 months in Health Care Centers from September 27, 2007 to May 12, 2008.

----------Shirley Christmas 2008

Shirley was home a month or two, and, started to have more problems with her feet. She was in and out of the Hospital several times since then. In December 2008 she was in the hospital for several days, and then, was placed in Westwood Health Care for 30 days.

Shirley's Last Birthday Party Jan.1, 2009 at IHOPS

On January 1, 2009 was her 74th birthday. They, always, celebrated her birthday, with a breakfast. Her Brother, Larry, was here with his family from Nebraska in late December and a few days in January. They signed Shirley out of the Health Care Center early, the morning of January 1st, and Larry's

family and, all of Sylvan and Shirley's family met at IHOPS for breakfast. They had a wonderful time, and, Shirley was delighted to be there, with her family, even if she did have to be in a Wheel Chair!

Several pictures were taken. I'm going to show you some of them here.

Inside of IHOPS

In front of IHOP

Shirley & Sylvan
With Larry & Carolyn

Larry's Family

The Bilby Family

Shirley & Liz, Shirley's Niece-------

That was Shirley's last Birthday!
A Sad, but, a Happy Affair

On, this, and the last page of this book I will try to give you a short description of Shirley's last few months here. After her wonderful birthday party, they took her back to the Health Care Center until the end of January. On Feb. 3, small facial skin cancers were treated by her skin doctor again. Her left foot was, still, in bad shape. She couldn't walk at all! Her regular Doctor sent her to a Vascular Doctor for treatment March 12. She went back to the same doctor June 19. She had to go back to the Hospital around the middle of June. She was back Home by the end of June. Sylvan tried to take care of her, him self, but he was still too weak to lift her. He could move her around in the wheel chair. Her feet were so bad she couldn't get out of bed by her self. She had to be lifted out of bed to be put in a wheel chair. She couldn't <u>even</u> get into a car <u>with</u> help. She had to be transported to the doctors by a bus van with a wheel chair lift most of 2009. Finally, out of desperation, they had to send her to the Destin Health Care Center on July 17 by the bus with the chair lift. <u>They</u> cared for her until she went to be with The Lord at 8:15 AM on August 6, 2009. Her Funeral Service was held at the Living Word Church in Navarre, Fl. On Monday August 10th 2009, With the Reverends Bobby J. Brown and Stanley Price Presiding. After the Service She was interred in the Beal Memorial Cemetery in Ft. Walton Beach, Fl.

Sylvan was with her for several hours every day at Destin Health Care.

Just before her death, Sylvan sang to her...

"NEVER IN A MILLION YEARS!"

ALSO, ON DISC., AT THE FUNERAL SERVICE

A <u>SAD</u> AFFAIR, BECAUSE OF HER DEATH, A

<u>HAPPY</u> AFFAIR... BECAUSE, SHE HAS NO MORE ACHE OR PAIN, SHE'S WITH <u>THE LORD</u>!

After 57 years Sylvan surely misses Shirley!

IF THIS TRUE LOVE STORY IS TOO WONDERFUL TO BE TRUE, BUT IT IS! AND YOU ENJOYED THE LOVE LIFE OF THIS WONDERFUL COUPLE, THEIR HAPPY TIMES, HARDSHIPS, SORROW AND FAITH IN THEIR LIVES...PLEASE TELL SOMEONE ELSE. WE WANT THE WORLD TO KNOW WHAT <u>TRUE</u> EVERLASTING LOVE AND GODS FAITH CAN DO FOR THEM!

GOD BLESS YOU!